HEADWAY

STUDENT'S BOOK

INTERMEDIATE

John & Liz Soars

Oxford University Press

	Structure	Use	Vocabulary	Skill	Topic
1	Present Simple (1) Present Continuous	To express habits and states To express an activity in progress To express temporary activities around the present	go—ing v. play with games and sports	Exploiting prior knowledge Skimming	A day in the life of a pop star
2	Present Simple (2) Like doing v. like to do	Verbs that rarely take the continuous Expressing general and specific likes	Television programmes	Scanning quickly for specific information	Television page of a newspaper
3	Past Simple Past Continuous	To express completed actions in the past To describe past activities	Keeping vocabulary records Money Holidays	Rearranging jumbled texts to develop awareness of text cohesion	A biography A court case
4	Could you . . . ? Would you . . . ? I'll . . . Shall I . . . ?	Polite requests Offering to do things	Nationality words, country, adjective, people	Reading for gist Summarizing	Racial prejudice
5	Will Going to	As an auxiliary of the future As a modal verb to express intention To express premeditated intention	Word formation -ed and -ing adjectives Dictionary work Word families	Inferring Summarizing	English food
6	What's . . . like? What does he look like? How is he? Comparative and superlative adjectives	Questions for general and specific descriptions Expressing preference	Describing character Positive and negative connotation Antonyms with prefixes and suffixes	Appreciating a poem Inferring	Conforming to society
7	Present Perfect Simple	To express experience To express unfinished past action To express present result of past action	Guessing the meaning of unknown words, via context, lists, and opposites	Rearranging jumbled texts to develop awareness of text cohesion	Setting up small business
8	Must/mustn't/have to Should/shouldn't Don't have to	To express strong obligation To express mild obligation To express absence of obligation	Injuries, causes and treatment Dictionary work	Exploiting topic sentences for speed reading and prediction	Keeping fit by running
9	First conditional Second conditional Zero conditional	To express real conditions To express unreal conditions To express conditions that are always true	Prioritizing features of a house	Intensive reading	A questionnaire to see how long you will live

Speaking		Listening		Writing	
Activity	**Topic**	**Skill**	**Topic**	**Activity**	**Focus**
Roleplay	Finding your way around a strange town	Listening for specific information Transferring information	American and Russian weekends	Form filling	Spoken v. written language Instructions on forms
Discussion	Plus, minus, and interest points of television	Predicting Listening for gist	Children in professional sport	Describing a person	Fact and opinion in descriptions Qualifying adverbs
Discussion	Disastrous holidays	Predicting Note taking	A disastrous holiday	Gap filling	Linking words
Discussion	Nationality stereotypes	Listening for gist Note taking	An old lady who travels the world	Writing a narrative	Past tenses to narrate and describe Linking devices Descriptive vocabulary
Cued dialogue	Arranging to meet	Listening for specific information	Life in China	A formal letter of enquiry	The organization and conventions of formal letters Salutations Formulas for different purposes
Discussion Discussion	Growing old Conforming to different human groups	Inferring Note taking and comparing information	Descriptions of people Descriptions of places	Punctuating a formal letter	Punctuation, organization and paragraphing of a formal letter
Roleplay	Negotiating a bank loan	Listening for specific information	A retired man talks about his life	Informal letters	Comparison of formal and informal letters Salutations Formulas for different purposes
Discussion	The ethics of the medical profession	Listening for specific information	First aid	Gap filling	Linking devices and expressions
Discussion Discussion	English and foreign proverbs What would you do in these situations?	Listening for specific information Transferring information Fact and opinion	Discussing a prospective house purchase	Describing a house	Fact and opinion in descriptions Prepositional phrases Imperial and Metric measures

Structure	Use	Vocabulary	Skill	Topic
10 *Can/can't/could/manage to/able to* *Can/could/do you mind/would you mind . . .?*	To express ability To express permission	Base and extreme adjectives Intensifying adverbs *very* and *absolutely*	Reading for specific information Summarizing	A 12-year-old girl at Oxford University
11 Present Perfect Continuous	To express unfinished past activity To express present result of past activity	Compound nouns: one word/ two words/hyphenated	Scanning Intensive reading	Raising money for charity
12 Present Continuous *Might* and *could*	To express future arrangements To express future possibility	Phrasal Verbs (1): the three main types Recognizing which type from a dictionary Identifying correct concept for multiple entry phrasal verbs	Topic sentences and prediction	Future settlements in space
13 Passive sentences Present Simple and Continuous. Past Simple and Continuous; Present Perfect; infinitives	To move the focus of a sentence to the object of an active sentence	Antonyms with prefixes Synonyms and connotation	Gist reading	The abuse of personal information stored on computers
14 Reported statements Reported commands Reported and Indirect Questions	To report direct speech and thoughts To report direct commands To report direct questions	Ways of speaking Verbs and adverbs to describe the way we talk	Comparing three newspapers' treatment of the same story for stylistic variations	The death of David Kennedy

Speaking

Activity	Topic
Roleplay Discussion	The case for and against educating children at home Your experiences in education
Cued dialogue	A reunion with a friend, and exchanging news
Discussion	Are you an optimist or a pessimist about the future?
Discussion	Plus, minus, and interest points on the role of computers
Roleplay	A current news story, with reporters and characters

Listening

Skill	Topic
Note taking	Educating children at home
Gist listening	Different charity appeals
Listening for gist Intensive listening	Our dying planet
Listening for gist Note taking	The exploitation of home-workers
Prediction Comparing information	An interview with a divorce lawyer

Writing

Activity	Focus
Rearranging jumbled letter of complaint	Text cohesion Paragraphing Opening and closing paragraphs of a formal letter
Comparing two letters for style, organization and content	Analysing formal style Vocabulary and attitude in formal letters
Sentence combination	Manipulating complex clauses to produce concise coherent writing
Gap filling	Linking devices and markers of opinion
Discursive writing	Words and phrases that present different sides of an argument, and list points in an argument

UNIT 1

Present Simple and Present Continuous

Present Simple: habits and states

PRESENTATION

Statistics

There is, of course, no such thing as the average British family, but statistical data can help us to understand a society and social trends.

Every year, official statistics based on questionnaires and surveys are published and these provide a lot of useful information on people's habits. This profile is based on one of their recent publications.

The average British family:
A STEREOTYPE

The average British family lives in a semi-detached house with a garden in the south of England. They own their house, which is situated in the suburbs of a large town. The house has three bedrooms. On average they have two children and a pet. The family drives a two-year-old Ford Cortina.

He works in the office of an engineering company for 40 hours a week and earns £200 per week. He starts at 9.00 in the morning and finishes at 5.30 in the evening. He goes to work by car, which takes him 20 minutes. He doesn't particularly like his job, but there are chances of promotion.

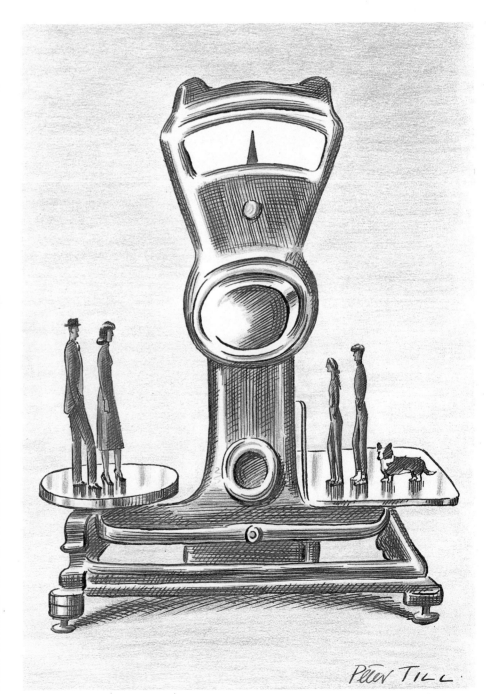

She works in a service industry for three days a week and earns £95. She works locally and goes there by bus. She quite likes her job as it gets her out of the house, she meets people, and it is close to the children's school.

───────

The children go to a state school which is a few miles from home. A special bus comes to pick them up every day. They are at school from 9.00 to 3.30.

───────

The most popular evening entertainment is watching television or video, which the average person does for two and a half hours a day. After that, the next most popular activity is visiting friends, going to the cinema or a restaurant, or going to the pub. The most popular hobby is gardening and the most popular sports are fishing, football and tennis.

● Grammar question

What tense are all the verbs in this profile? Why?

PRACTICE

Pairwork

1 Ask and answer questions about this family.
   Use:
   Where?/What?/When?/How?/
   How much?/How many?/
   Do . . . ?/Does . . . ?

   Example
   Q *Where does the family live?*
   A *In the south of England.*
   Q *What sort of car do they drive?*
   A *A Ford Cortina.*

2 Compare the British family with an average family from your country. Think of the following:
   house/jobs/hours of work/school/
   transport/entertainment

   Example
   In my country most people live in flats. School starts at 8.00, not at 9.00, and finishes at 1.00.

● Language review 1

The Present Simple: Uses

1 To express an action which happens again and again, that is, a *habit*.
   It is often found with these time expressions: always/every day/
   often/sometimes/never

   He always goes to work by car.
   They sometimes watch television in the evening.

2 To express a fact that stays the same for a long time, that is, a *state*.
   She lives in Madrid.
   I work in a bank.

Translate

I go to work by car.

We don't get up early on Saturdays.

What newspaper do you read?

◀ **Look back** at page 1 and underline the examples of the *Present Simple*.

Present Continuous: activities in progress

PRESENTATION

A journalist is interviewing Mr Williams about his job.
| **T.1** | Listen to the interview and fill in the chart.

Name	Occupation	Details of occupation	Present activity
Mr Williams			

● Grammar question

What is the difference between the *Present Simple* and the *Present Continuous*?

PRACTICE

Pairwork

Make up dialogues like this using the prompts below.
A What do you do?
B I'm an interior designer. I decorate people's houses, and give them ideas for the furniture and the lighting.
A And what are you doing at the moment?
B I'm designing the reception at the Hilton Hotel.

member of the European Parliament/
architect/journalist/inventor/
commercial artist/astronomer

Listen

On a separate piece of paper, draw a chart like the one for Mr Williams. The journalist is interviewing someone else about his job.
| **T.2** | Listen and fill in your chart.

● Language review 2

The Present Continuous: Uses

1 To express an activity that is in progress **now**.
   I'm reading this book at the moment.
   Peter's sitting next to me.

2 To express an activity happening for a limited period of time *around now*.

I normally come to work by car, but my car's broken down, so I'm coming to work by train this week. What's your brother doing these days?

Translate

I'm reading a book at the moment.

_____

_____

They aren't working.

_____

What are you doing?

_____

◀ **Look back** at page 2 and underline the examples of the *Present Continuous*.

▶ **Grammar reference** page 87.

SKILLS DEVELOPMENT
● Listening

Pre-listening task

In pairs, ask and answer questions about the weekend.

Examples
What do you usually do at the weekend?
Do you have a routine?
Do you play any sports?

Listening for specific information

T.3 Listen to these two people talking about their weekends. While you are listening, find the answers to the questions and fill in the chart like this:

√ = Yes   X = No   ? = I don't know

	1 Is he/she busy?	2 Does he/she do any sport?	3 Does he/she like the weekend?
Harry			
Svetlana			

Listen to the tape again, and for each person write down three things that he or she does at the weekend. Compare your lists with a partner. Whose weekend is most like your own?

● Vocabulary

Group Work

1 Make a list of as many sports and leisure activities as you can think of. These symbols will help you.

Notice the different verbs:
play

*I **play** golf with friends.*
*She **plays** squash very well.*

These are sports, played with a ball.

go

*I **go** horse-riding every Sunday.*
*They **go** skiing in winter.*

These are sports or leisure activities.

2 On a separate piece of paper draw columns. Choose some of the sports or activities from your list and fill in the columns like this.

3 Work in pairs. Ask and answer questions like these:
What sports do you play?
How often . . . ?
Where . . . ?
Are you good at . . . ?

sport	go or play?	person	place	equipment needed
football	*play*	*footballer*	*football ground*	*ball and boots*

A LIFE IN THE DAY OF

LINDA McCARTNEY

"We live in a two-bedroom house so as soon as James (2) starts calling 'Mummy, Mummy', around seven every morning, he wakes everyone up. Being his mother I like to be the first to greet him, so up I get.

I take him downstairs and start getting breakfast ready. Before long the other kids — Heather (almost 17), Mary (10) and Stella (8) — are also down. If Paul is recording or we are touring I try to make sure he's not disturbed. But if he isn't working he gets up at the same time and joins the kids at breakfast. He's an excellent father, very involved and protective towards them.

It seems mad to have moved from a large house in London to a small place on the South Coast, but it's so much cosier. Paul and I are in the kind of business where we can be totally detached from our kids and hardly see them grow up. If you have enough money to live in a big house, one kid could be up in the attic and another could be in the west wing and you'd hardly see them.

The kids travel everywhere with us. When touring abroad we usually rent a house and make it our base so we can return to the kids each night.

We're all vegetarian, so breakfast is eggs laid by our own hens, home-grown tomatoes fried, vegetarian sausages, cereals and wholewheat bread. During the bread strike Paul baked the most beautiful bread!

Quite often Paul comes with me when I drive the girls to school. Mary and Stella go to a local primary school and Heather attends a nearby art school. I drive a Mini because being American I'm used to wide roads, so with a small car I've no fear about scraping it.

I buy most of the kids' clothes at Mothercare. I look at their catalogue or go into the shop and pick out things that are made from natural fibres. I myself feel most comfortable in jeans and T-shirt. I don't really spend that much — even though Paul pays all the bills! Because we live locally I'm regarded as just another mother who takes her children to school and has a house to keep. I try to keep my life close to what it was before we married.

Because we have a big break-fast and a big dinner about six we don't have lunch. So about that time I'm doing jobs around the house. Paul never helps me. He likes tidiness but is not too tidy himself! If I'm working or going out I have a woman in to do the cleaning. But I always do the cooking because I enjoy it. I cook for six every day.

For dinner I make things like quiche Lorraine — without bacon — aubergines, spaghetti, salads and Paul's favourites which are pea soup or cream of tomato soup made from home-grown tomatoes and onions. I also make coffee milkshakes which I love. I'm a real baby that way!

If I'm lucky during the day I go for a ride on my stallion called Lucky Spot. He's got a lovely temperament. Horse riding is a marvellous form of exercise, both physically and spiritually.

One interest we share closely is football. We rarely get to see matches but we always watch it on television. Paul is a great Liverpool fan, so we support Liverpool.

Because we live in the country we don't socialize that much. We think that's also partly because we're too lazy. There's so much I'd like to do, especially in the photographic field, but I hate to leave the life I lead in the country unless I absolutely have to.

I get various offers to take photographs, and sometimes I might find one particularly attractive. But when it comes down to it I just can't bring myself to leave the kids and go to take pictures. So I stay at home and take pictures of them instead.

Most of our evenings are spent in front of the television. I watch *Dallas*, *Top of the Pops*, *Old Grey Whistle Test* and some quiz shows.

Before I turn in for the night I always go to the kid's bedroom and give them each a kiss. Trouble is, James often wakes up and doesn't want to go back to sleep."

Reading

A life in the day of . . .
'A life in the day of' is a feature which appears in the *Sunday Times* newspaper every week. Well-known people describe an ordinary day in their life, and they talk about their habits and routines, their family and their work.

The article opposite is about Linda McCartney, the wife of Paul McCartney, who was one of the members of the Beatles in the 1960s and 1970s.

Pre-reading task
1 What do you already know about Linda McCartney?
2 Look at the picture. What does it tell you about Linda? Fill in the columns opposite with as much information as you can.
3 What do you want to know from the article?
Write questions about Linda like these:
When does she get up?
What clothes . . . ?
Ask about the following topics.
Daily routine: food/hobbies/car
Family life: children/home/school
Work: what?/where?/how often?

Reading for specific information
Read the article. Try to find the answers to your questions. Don't worry about any words you don't know.

Comprehension check
Work in pairs.
1 Which of your questions did you find the answers to? Read the text again if necessary.
2 Did you have any questions that weren't answered? Can you guess the answers?

What do you think?
1 Do you think Linda is happy in her life? Why?
2 What do you think takes up most of Linda's days?

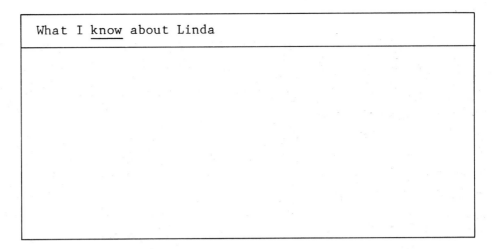

```
What I know about Linda
```

```
What I think I know, but I'm not sure of
```

Of course we don't know exactly, because the article does not give us all the information. But we can guess.

If you think Linda spends most of her time gardening, put 1 in the box next to Gardening.

☐ Riding
☐ Cooking
☐ Looking after her children
☐ Taking photographs
☐ Gardening
☐ Doing the housework
☐ Watching television
☐ Visiting friends

3 Is there anything in the article that surprises you?

Example
They have four children but they live in a house with only two bedrooms.

Speaking

Roleplay

Student A You have just arrived in London for the first time.

You have come for a holiday and to learn English. London seems a little strange and you need to ask for help.

These are some of your problems:
1 You need to change some travellers' cheques, but you don't know where to find a bank, or what time the banks open and close.
2 You need to buy some stamps and postcards.
3 You would like to buy a newspaper from your country.
4 You want to find a good English language school.

You meet someone who lives in London and who seems friendly, so you ask for information. Prepare what you are going to say. Add any other questions you want to ask. (E.g. about accommodation, shops, etc.).

Begin like this:
Excuse me. Could you help me, please?

Student B You live in London and know it quite well. You meet a foreigner who has just arrived, and who seems to have some problems. Look at the information here and try to help him/her.

Barclays Bank

Opening hours
Mon–Fri 9.30–3.30
Closed all day Saturday

HIGH STREET POST OFFICE

Opening hours

Mon	9.00–5.30
Tues	9.00–5.30
Wed	9.00–1.00
Thurs	9.00–5.30
Fri	9.00–5.30
Sat	9.00–1.00

BLOCK CAPITALS

Surname (Mr/Mrs/Miss/Ms*)_____
First name_____
Date of birth_____
Place of birth_____
Marital status_____

Present address_____

Permanent address (if different from above)_____
_____

Hobbies/interests_____
Present occupation   Student/employee/self-employed/other*
If other, state present occupation_____

*Delete where not applicable

For office use only

Signed_____

Writing

Form filling

Look at the form. How does it ask these questions?
1 When were you born?
2 Where were you born?
3 Are you married?
4 What's your job?

Fill in the form, but first make sure you understand these terms.
BLOCK CAPITALS
Delete where not applicable

UNIT 2

Present Simple (2)

Expressing likes

PRESENTATION

Willi Hoffman is a member of the European Parliament. He represents the Christian Democratic party, and comes from Hanover. He has three children. He speaks fluent English and French, and a little Russian. He lists his interests as history, literature and music.

The information in this *Fact File* comes from a recent biography.

● Grammar question

What's the difference between the following two sentences?

I like going to the theatre.
I'd like to go to the theatre.

PRACTICE

Write three facts about Willi Hoffman's life.

Example

He comes from Hanover.

_____

_____

_____

Write two of his political opinions.

_____

_____

FACT FILE   WILLI HOFFMAN

Politics
Conservative. He wants Germany's economy to be strong again, and he hopes that higher productivity will increase exports. He believes in nuclear power and thinks that nuclear weapons are necessary to keep world peace.

Work habits
He needs very little sleep, only four hours a night, and says he works at least twelve hours a day.

Entertainment
He likes going to the theatre and watching television, but he is often too busy.

Ambitions
He'd like to stay in politics for as long as possible, and one day he'd like to write his autobiography.

Pairwork

1 Write a similar profile about a politician, real or imaginary. Include information for these topics:
– Facts about his or her life
– Political opinions
– Work habits
– Entertainment
– Ambitions

2 Make up dialogues, using the prompts below.

Example

– a cigarette

A *Would you like a cigarette?*
B *No thanks. I don't smoke.*

– go to the cinema

A *Would you like to go to the cinema?*
B *Yes, I would. / Yes, I'd love to.*

– a drink
– something to eat
– go out for a meal
– an ice-cream
– go horse-riding this weekend
– come to a party on Saturday
– a piece of chewing gum
– have a look at my newspaper

Listen

T.4 Les Mickleby is talking about his job.
On a separate piece of paper, write down

1 what he likes about his job.
2 what he dislikes about his job.
3 what you think his job is.

● Language review 1

Certain verbs are almost never used in the *Present Continuous*.

hope   think   like
believe   need   want

◄**Look back** at page 7. Find these verbs and underline them.

● Language review 2

Expressing likes

1 Generally or Always
I like dancing. (like + gerund)
I like English. (like + noun)

2 Now or at a Specific time
I'd like to dance.
(would + like + infinitive)
I'd like a drink.
(would + like + noun)

Translate

Do you like watching television?

_____

Yes, I do.

_____

Would you like to watch television?

_____

Yes, I would.

◄**Look back** again at page 7. Underline the examples of *like* and *would like*.

SKILLS DEVELOPMENT
● Vocabulary

Television

1 How many TV channels are there in your country?
2 Is there any difference between them?
3 What kinds of programme do you like watching?

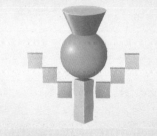

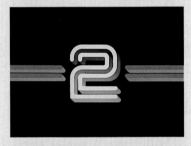

Look at these descriptions of different types of TV programmes. What kinds of programme are they? Match them with one of the words below. Mark it like this.

1 ☑d Boxing from the Albert Hall and racing from York.
2 ☐ A new production of Shakespeare's Richard III at the Lyric Theatre, London.
3 ☐ Cagney and Lacey as the American cops. In this week's episode they're chasing heroin dealers.
4 ☐ Geoff Hamilton is in the garden, telling us what to do at this time of year.
5 ☐ This week's top twenty, with disc jockey Mike Reid.
6 ☐ A laugh a minute as the northern comedian Les Dawson entertains.
7 ☐ More adventures from Disneyland with Donald Duck.
8 ☐ Superb filming in this programme about the disappearing forests of South America. Will the world continue to have oxygen?
9 ☐ More families try to answer the questions and win fabulous prizes, with host Lesley Crowther.
10 ☐ Terry Wogan's guests tonight belong to the sporting, theatrical, and business worlds.
11 ☐ Tomorrow's weather.
12 ☐ The Magnificent Seven. 1960 classic western starring Yul Brynner, Steve McQueen, and Charles Bronson.

a. a music programme
b. a detective story
c. a cartoon
d. a sports programme
e. a film
f. a quiz
g. a play
h. a chat show
i. a comedy
j. weather forecast
k. a documentary
l. a gardening programme

BBC 1

6.30 Breakfast Time: Today's presenters are Selina Scott and Frank Bough. News headlines at 6.30, 7.00, 7.30, 8.00 and 8.30. Headlines on the quarter hours, and regional news and traffic at 6.45, 7.15, 7.45 and 8.15. Today's guests, Peter Ustinov and Harold Macmillan, will be talking about the Soviet Union.

12.30 News After Noon: and weather prospects; **12.57 Financial Report.** And news headlines, with sub-titles.

1.00 Pebble Mill at One: the conversation and music magazine from the studio foyer.

1.45 Postman Pat: puppet story for the youngsters.

2.00 American Gardens: A non-commentary, pictures-and-music "filler" rather like the soothing potters wheel "fillers" of old.

2.15 Racing from Newbury: Featuring the big race of the day – the Gainsborough Stud Fred Darling Stakes, at 3.00. We also see the 2.30 and 3.30 races. Commentary by Julian Wilson.

3.55 Play School: (also on BBC 2, at 11.00am); **4.20 The New Schmoo:** cartoon; **4.40 The Unknown Enchantment:** by Rosemary Harris. The story of the casting of a spell.

5.10 Breakthrough: New series begins. John Craven tells the story of Edward Jenner, the humble village doctor who made the first important discovery about smallpox. He visits Jenner's house at Berkeley.

5.35 Roobarb (r).

5.40 News: and weather prospects; **6.00 South East at Six; 6.22 Nationwide:** including Sportswide at 6.45.

7.00 Film: A Gathering of Eagles (1962) Drama about the United States's Strategic Air Command in the nuclear age, with Rock Hudson as the efficiency-obsessed colonel who gives others at his command base a very trying time.

9.00 News: and weekend weather prospects.

9.25 Cagney and Lacey: American-made drama series about two policewomen. Tonight, the authorities allow a master jewel thief to slip through their fingers. He is an elderly gentleman, arrested on a minor charge and released on bail.

10.15 Happy Endings: Another view of life composed by Peter Skellern in a blend of music and comedy. The last in the present repeated series (r).

10.45 News headlines: and weather prospects for the weekend.

10.50 Film: Valdez is Coming (1971) Conventional Western about a Mexican lawman who kills a suspect and tries to make amends by caring for the widow.

ITV/LONDON

9.30 Sesame Street: learning things, with The Muppets; **10.30 Science International:** facts for Everyman; **10.35 The Poseidon Files:** The hunt for the humpback whale; **11.30 Film Fun:** Compilation of award-winning Warner Brothers cartoons, presented by Derek Griffiths (r).

12.00 Topper's Tales: with Julian Orchard (r); **12.10 Rainbow:** with Gerry Marsden as guest; **12.30 Wild, Wild, World of Animals:** The clever tricks of the racoon's cousin, the Coati Mundi.

1.00 News from ITN.

2.00 A Plus: The topic is middle age. A studio audience discuss it with writers Molly Parkin and Christopher Matthews.

2.30 Film: Too Many Crooks (1958*) Engaging British comedy about a gang of bungling kidnappers. With Terry-Thomas, George Cole, Sidney James and Vera Day. Director: Mario Zampi.

4.00 Children's ITV: Rainbow (r); **4.20 Dangermouse:** the cartoon series that is now selling well in video form; **4.25 Animals in Action:** All sorts and conditions of frogs.

4.50 Freetime: Youngsters perform songs they have written.

5.15 Make Me Laugh. A chuckle-provoking contest.

5.45 News; 6.00 The 6 o'clock Show: The lighter side of the news, with Michael Aspel and Janet Street-Porter.

7.00 Family Fortunes: Prize and cash quiz, with Bob Monkhouse. The Browns from Airdrie take on the Ladds from Romford, Essex.

7.30 Hawaii Five-O: Steve Garrett suspects that a doctor is illegally supplying drugs to addicts.

8.30 Pig in the Middle: Susan embraces her new-found freedom and Barty begins to feel trapped.

9.00 Death of an Expert Witness: Episode 2 of Robin Chapman's dramatization of the P D James murder story reveals the private, poetic side of Adam Dalgliesh of the Yard (Roy Marsden). And Maxim Howarth (Barry Foster) starts work as the new director of the scientific team at Hoggatt's forensic laboratory.

10.00 News at Ten.

10.30 The London Programme: Islington Council has earned for itself the name of "the Bananas Republic" because of the odd subjects that end up on the agenda for debate by its left-wing members. We learn tonight why the council has rivalled the GLC for the column inches it has won in the newspapers.

11.00 Shoot Pool! The second match in the John Bull Bitter London Pool Championships has Charlie Nolan competing against Raymond Farrbrother.

BBC 2

6.05 Open University. Until 8.10. Maths Methods: linear equations; 6.30 Beneath Scotland; 6.55 Engineering Statics; 7.20 Quantum: Theory and atomic structure; 7.45 Molluscan evolution.

11.00 Play School: also on BBC 1, at 3.55. Closedown at 11.25.

5.10 ABC in Kansas City: The last of four films in ABC's coverage of the 1976 Republican Convention in Kansas City.

5.35 Weekend Outlook. Open University preview.

5.40 Film: A Date with the Falcon (1941*). Modestly made thriller starring George Sanders at his immaculate best. It is the story of a famous scientist who disappears. Co-starring Wendy Barrie.

6.40 Cameo: a short pictorial essay.

6.50 Madhur Jaffrey's Indian Cookery: Rogan Josh.

7.15 News summary. With sub-titles.

7.20 Headingley Test: How a cricket wicket is made. The story of Keith Boyce, head groundsman at Headingley whose job is to prepare all 20 wickets on the square. But much of his skill and energy is reserved for wicket number 12 – the Test wicket. We learn how, in the summer of 1981, wicket 12 went badly wrong.

7.50 Did You See . . .? A panel (Margaret Jay, Bernard Ashley and Yusuf Hassan) discuss Tucker's Luck, 20-20 Vision (the Channel 4 programme about punters) and Village Earth. And Miles Kington talks about doctors and nurses on television. The presenter: Iain Johnstone.

8.35 Gardeners' World: Kenneth and Gillain Beckett write books and their garden at Stanhoe, Norfolk not only gives them interest and pleasure but also provides them with living reference material. Roy Lancaster and Geoff Hamilton visit the garden.

9.00 Entertainment USA: Jonathan King, in New York City, looks at life and entertainment in America. Items include star interviews, a review of American television, and a report on local radio, American-style. First in a new eight-week series.

9.30 Guests of the Nation: Maurice Leitch's adaptation of Frank O'Connor's classic Irish short story set in County Cork in 1920. Starring Timothy Spall and Tim Woodward. (See Choice)

10.25 Newsnight: comment and news bulletins.

11.15 The Old Grey Whistle Test: Recorded in Dortmund, Germany, this "rock-pop in" concert features Gary Moore and R.E.O. Speedwagon. Can be seen again on April 19. Ends at midnight.

CHANNEL 4

5.15 Acting with Anna: The disciplined play techniques that are perfected at Anna Scher's children's theatre in Islington are demonstrated in this, the first of six films about a remarkable school devoted to what Miss Scher calls "fact-finding".

5.30 Countdown: Word quiz game, presented by Richard Whiteley and Kenneth Williams.

6.00 Switch: The show that is aimed directly at the pop music generation. Includes a location report by Marc Issue, and music from Alison (Alf) Moyet and Orange Juice.

7.00 Channel Four News: News and comment.

7.30 The Friday Alternative: Sharp focus on Asians and blacks in Leicester – their feelings about the white community in the city in general and why they think that, in some respects, (culture and business success) they are sometimes superior to the local whites.

8.00 What a Picture: First in new series intended to help the amateur photographer to take better pictures. The tutor is John Hedgecoe, Professor of Photography at the Royal College of Art.

8.30 Jazz on Four: Joint recital at the Royal Albert Hall by three masters of the guitar: John McLaughlin, Larry Coryell and Paco de Lucia.

9.30 Capstick Capers: Jokes and stories from the comedian and singer Tony Capstick. He is supported by the Carleton Main Frickley Colliery Band. The setting is a club where Mr Capstick's "twin brother" also works.

10.00 Cheers: A timid young priest-to-be makes amorous advances towards Diane, the girl in the American saloon bar.

10.30 Predicaments: Mavis Nicholson encourages a group of ordinary people to discuss their feelings about the prospect of impending death. This is the ninth programme in what has become a compelling series which has gained much from Miss Nicholson's committed interviewing technique.

11.15 Film: The Big Shot (1942*). Modestly budgeted thriller with Humphrey Bogart as the gangster who tries to go straight but is then caught up in a criminal enterprise masterminded by a lawyer. It was Bogart's last B-movie for Warner Brothers, the company for whom he made his best films and it was made in the same year that he appeared in Casablanca. The film co-stars Irene Manning, Richard Travis, Susan Peters, and Stanley Ridges (as the lawyer). Directed by Lewis Seiler. Ends at 12.45.

Reading

Scan Reading

'Scan reading' means reading quickly to find specific information.

You don't have to read every word. This is how you read a telephone directory or a train timetable.

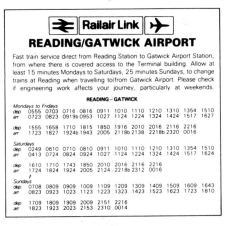

≷ Railair Link ✈
READING/GATWICK AIRPORT

Fast train service direct from Reading Station to Gatwick Airport Station, from where there is covered access to the Terminal building. Allow at least 15 minutes Mondays to Saturdays, 25 minutes Sundays, to change trains at Reading when travelling to/from Gatwick Airport. Please check if engineering work affects your journey, particularly at weekends.

READING – GATWICK

Mondays to Fridays

dep	0555	0703	0716	0816	0911	1010	1110	1210	1310	1354	1510
arr	0723	0823	0919b	0953	1027	1124	1224	1324	1424	1517	1627
dep	1555	1658	1710	1815	1850	1916	2010	2016	2116	2216	
arr	1723	1827	1924b	1943	2005	2118b	2138	2218b	2320	0016	

Saturdays

dep	0249	0610	0710	0810	0911	1010	1110	1210	1310	1354	1510
arr	0413	0724	0824	0924	1027	1124	1224	1324	1424	1517	1627
dep	1610	1710	1743	1850	2010	2016	2116	2216			
arr	1724	1824	1924	2005	2124	2218b	2312	0016			

Sundays

dep	0708	0809	0909	1009	1109	1209	1309	1409	1509	1609	1643
arr	0823	0923	1023	1123	1223	1323	1423	1523	1623	1723	1810
dep	1709	1809	1909	2009	2151	2216					
arr	1823	1923	2023	2153	2310	0014					

Work in pairs.
You are going to look at a page from a British newspaper which gives the television programmes for one day.

Answer the questions as quickly as possible. This is a competition. See who can finish first.

1 How many films are on?
2 Which film would you recommend to someone who likes westerns?
3 If you like taking photographs, which programme should you watch?
4 What music programmes are on? Which channel?
5 Are there any cartoons?
6 Is there a comedy programme on between 9.00 and 10.00?
7 How many times can you see the news?
8 If you like gardening or cooking, which channel should you watch?
9 What sort of programme is the Friday Alternative, Channel 4 at 7.30?
10 Which channel ends first? Which channel ends last?

Pairwork

You live in the same house, and there is only one television. Talk together and decide what to watch tonight.

Speaking

Discussion

How important is television to you? Answer these questions honestly!

1 On average, how many hours a week do you watch television?
2 'Television is chewing-gum for the eyes.' Do you sometimes watch television because you have nothing better to do?
3 Do you watch television selectively? Or do you often turn off the television only when you go to bed?

Group work

What are the good points and bad points about television?
On a separate piece of paper draw two columns and add to this list:

```
Good points

It keeps you informed
about the rest of the
world.
```

```
Bad points

It stops people talking.
```

Can you think of any *interest* points, that is, neither good nor bad?

```
Interest points

In some countries there is
no television for one or
two days a week.
```

T.5 Here are the first words of a
radio programme.
'On today's programme we look at
the children who are trying to be
champions in the world of sport, and
the pressures they can be under to
win, win, win.'

Pre-listening task

1 In which sports do children compete with adults?

2 What do you think the pressures mentioned in the introduction are? Where do they come from?

3 Do you expect the programme will
- give advice to children about how to become professional?
- suggest that children should *not* become professional?
- say that children should specialize as early as possible?
- say that children should live a normal life?

Listening for gist

'Gist' means general, most important information .
Listen to the rest of the interview.
See if any of your ideas are discussed.

Comprehension check

1 What is the advantage for a child to begin a sport at a young age? What is the disadvantage?

2 What happens at a tennis school in America?

3 What is Pam de Gruchy's advice to young tennis players?

4 What is Robert's ambition?

5 What are some of the things he likes doing?

What do you think?

1 Do you agree with Pam de Gruchy's advice to teenage tennis players? Do you think they'll be better tennis players than the Americans?
In your opinion, should there be a minimum age for teenagers becoming professional?

2 Different countries have reputations for being good at different sports. Can you think of some examples?

Example
The East Germans are very good at athletics.

Why, do you think?

3 Think of some children who have excelled in the world of sport, music (classical and pop), art, films and entertainment.
How were they affected by their success and fame?

Writing

Describing a person

Of all my relatives, I like my Aunt Emily the best. She's my mother's youngest sister. She has never married, and lives alone in a small village near Bath. She's in her late fifties, but she's quite young in spirit. She has a fair complexion, thick brown hair which she wears in a bun, and dark brown eyes. She has a kind face, and when you meet her, the first thing you notice is her smile. Her face is a little wrinkled now, but I think she is still rather attractive. She is the sort of person you can always go to if you have a problem.

She likes reading and gardening, and she still goes for long walks over the hills. She's a very active person. Either she's making something, or mending something, or doing something to entertain herself. She's extremely generous, but not very tolerant with people who don't agree with her. I hope I'm as contented as she is when I'm her age.

1 The text consists of *factual description* and *personal opinions*. Go through the text and underline like this _____ what is factual description, and like this _ _ _ _ _ what is personal opinion.

2 Go through the text again and say which parts describe
- her face and body
- her character
- her likes and dislikes
- her habits
Sometimes the same sentence will describe two of these.

3 List the adjectives used in the text, and say if they describe the person's character or appearance.

4 Sometimes an adjective is qualified. For example, the text says she isn't 'very tolerant'. Find the other examples where adjectives are qualified.

5 'She isn't very tolerant.' This is a nice way of saying 'she is intolerant'. Sometimes we avoid saying a negative quality by saying 'not very' + the opposite adjective. How could you tactfully describe someone who is cruel/ mean/rude/stupid/boring?

6 Who is 'you' in the text?

7 Notice the verbs used in the text. For example, 'She*'s* my mother's youngest sister', 'she*'s got* grey hair', 'she *has* a kind face', etc. ('*She's got*' and '*she has*' mean the same thing.)

Now write a similar description of someone you know. Include the following:
- physical facts and description
- character, likes and dislikes, habits
- your opinions.

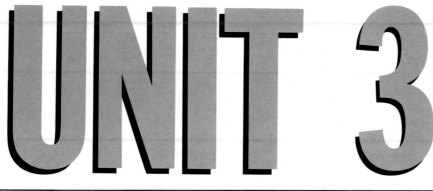

Past Simple and Past Continuous

Narrating past events

PRESENTATION

Unfortunately this is a *true* story. In January 1978 the firemen were on strike, and the army took over the job of answering emergency calls.

1 Here is a list of verbs in the *Past Simple* which tell the events of the story.
Look at the pictures and put the verbs in the right order.
Number them 1–10.

- [ ] rescued
- [ ] arrived
- [ ] climbed
- [ ] killed
- [ ] called
- [ ] invited
- [ ] couldn't get down
- [ ] ran over
- [ ] put up (the ladder)
- [ ] offered

2 Here is a list of verbs in the *Past Continuous* which describe the scene of the narrative.
Look at the pictures and put the verbs in the right order.
Letter them a–d.

- [ ] was waiting
- [ ] were leaving
- [ ] was working
- [ ] was playing

3 Now complete the story about Mrs Brewin by putting a number or a letter into each gap.

On 14 January 1978 Mrs Brewin
_____ in her garden. Her cat,

Henry, _____ around her. It _____
a tree in the garden and _____, so
she _____ the Fire Brigade. While
she _____ for them to arrive, she
_____ him some fish to try to get
him down.

The army finally _____, _____
their ladder and _____ the cat.
Mrs Brewin was delighted and
_____ them in for some tea. But as
they _____ ten minutes later, they
_____ the cat and _____ it.

● Grammar Question

What is the difference between the
Past Simple and the *Past Continuous?*

PRACTICE

Pairwork

Talk about your last holiday.

Student A asks the questions.

For example:
Where did you go?
Where . . .?/How long . . .?/What
. . .?/Where . . .?/Did . . .?

Student B replies.

For example:
I went to America.

Then change.
Ask about: the weather/the food/the
people.

Listen

| **T.6** | Listen to these three short
recordings. There are no words, but
you can hear various noises. For
each tape write *what was happening*
(×3) and finally *what happened* (×1).

Look at the example.

Tape 1

Describe the situation

The wind was blowing.

_____

_____

What happened?

_____

Tape 2

Describe the situation

_____

_____

What happened?

_____

Tape 3

Describe the situation.

_____

_____

What happened?

_____

● Language review 1

The Past Simple: Use

The *Past Simple* is used to express an
action
– in the **past**
– at a **specific time**
– which is **now finished**

Look at the time expressions which
are used with this tense.

| I did it | yesterday.
| | last week.
| | at 9.00 this morning.
| | in 1983.

Translate

I went to America last year.

_____

Where did you stay?

_____

We didn't buy anything.

_____

◀**Look back** at pages 14 and 15 and
underline the examples of the *Past
Simple.*

● Language review 2

The Past Continuous: Use

The *Past Continuous* is used to
describe a situation in the past. As
with all continuous tenses (*see page
88*) there is the idea of *duration* and
activity, and the activity is seen **in
progress.**

*When I arrived, she **was making**
some coffee.*

Translate

When I arrived, she was making
some coffee.

_____

When I arrived, she made some
coffee.

15

◀ **Look back** at page 14 and 15 underline the examples of the *Past Continuous*.

▶ Grammar reference page 89.

SKILLS DEVELOPMENT
⬤ Reading

Arranging jumbled text

1 On this page there are two newspaper stories, but they have been mixed up.
Look at the headlines.
Read the paragraphs quickly and first decide which paragraphs go with which story.

2 Put the paragraphs in the right order.
Mary

1 b	4 i	7 n
2 d	5 k	8 p
3 f	6 m	9 e

Housewife

1 a	3 j	5 l	7 o
2 h	4 g	6 c	

Comprehension check/Language work

Work in pairs.
Here are the *answers* to some questions.
Work out the *question*.

Mary
1 Sixty.
2 One hundred and three.
3 When she was six weeks old.
4 For 11 years.
5 She worked as a nurse.
6 In 1961.
7 For twenty-two years.
8 Yes, she does. But someone helps her as well.

Housewife
1 £11,922.
2 £32 a week.
3 Because she wanted to buy a caravan.

Wife who could not stop spending

Mary will not be giving up smoking...

a. A HOUSEWIFE who went on an £11,922 three-year spending spree complained in the London Bankruptcy Court yesterday that credit was far too easy to get. 'There ought to be a law to change these things,' she told the court. 'It's so easy, you just go on and on.'

b. Mary Padley smokes 60 cigarettes a day, plus the odd Churchill-sized cigar—and she is not giving up for anyone.

c. 'Every time I got a monthly statement it always said: '"Why don't you increase your credit limit".'

d. Even her doctor admits there is no point asking her to stop. Mrs Padley has just celebrated her 103rd birthday.

e. Her recipe for long life is 'work hard and don't think too much about tomorrow'.

f. She planned a small lunch party. But forty guests turned up and stayed until midnight.

g. She said all she had left now were assets worth £92. She had filed her own petition for bankruptcy because she 'didn't know how to solve the problem'.

h. Mrs Linda Smaje, 39, who earns £32 a week as a domestic worker, and whose husband is unemployed, used finance companies and big-store credit cards to buy presents for her children and furnishings for her home.

i. Mrs Padley saw little of the outside world till she was 28. Orphaned at six weeks, she was raised by nuns in Ireland and at 17 joined the very strict Poor Clare order. She left at 28.

j. Outside court Mrs Smaje complained that the stores and finance companies continually tempted her to go on spending. 'They never checked my credit-worthiness. They always said "of course you can have the money".'

k. 'My goodness was I innocent,' she recalls. 'Apart from a few priests, I had never seen a man. I knew nothing at all about life.'

l. Questioned by Mr Albert Billing, Assistant Official Receiver, she said she started opening bank accounts, applying for credit cards, and generally getting credit in 1979. In March 1980 she obtained a £1,640 loan to buy a caravan. Then she borrowed £2,000 elsewhere for kitchen equipment she did not really need.

m. She moved to London, where she worked as a maid and cook. She was a nurse during the First World War and an air-raid warden in the Second, crawling out of bomb debris on four occasions.

n. She married fellow warden Frederick Padley in 1939. He died in 1961 aged 72.

o. 'I blame the London stores who encouraged me to spend and spend. I just had to pick up the telephone and ask for more, and their salesman replied: "Of course, madam".'

p. Nowadays Mrs Padley has a home help, but likes doing her own housework and bakes all her own cakes. She used to tend two gardens until Age Concern stopped her digging up last year's potato crops.

Vocabulary

In the story about the wife who couldn't stop spending there are a lot of words to do with money.
On a separate piece of paper draw columns like this.

Read the article again and put the words related to money in the appropriate columns.
Use your dictionary to check the meaning of any unknown words.

Verb	Noun	Expression
to spend to earn	bankruptcy	to open a bank account

Listening

Pre-listening task: Dictionary work

Find out the meaning and pronunciation of the following words:

disastrous   to be sick
to have a row   to hitchhike
a war   to get a lift
a charter flight   a vineyard
to freeze   a maniac

You can hear all these words in the following listening text.
Before you listen, discuss in pairs what you think the story could be about. The title is *A Disastrous Holiday*.

Listening for gist

T.7 There are five disasters listed in the story. While you listen, make notes on each one.

Comprehension check

Are these statements true or false?
Put T (True) or F (False) in the box.

1 ☐ The holiday was disastrous because John and Susan argued all the time.
2 ☐ Italy was their second choice for a holiday.
3 ☐ They missed the flight because they arrived late at the airport.
4 ☐ Their friend Peter helped them after they missed the flight.
5 ☐ They tried to book another flight.
6 ☐ They started hitching in the early morning.
7 ☐ It took a long time to get a lift.
8 ☐ They were happy after meeting a man who owned a vineyard.
9 ☐ Susan was sick in someone's car.

Language work

Complete these sentences:
1 They _____ in the bar when the plane _____.
2 It was difficult to get out of Paris because a lot of other people _____.
3 When Susan pretended to be sick, the driver _____, and John and Susan _____.

Speaking

Discussion

In pairs, make a list of as much vocabulary to do with holidays as you can think of.

For example:
to book a holiday/to pack/to cancel a flight/to check in

Talk about a disastrous holiday of yours.

These questions will help you:
1 When was it?
2 Who were you with?
3 What went wrong?
4 How did it happen?
5 What happened next?
6 What happened in the end?

Writing

Linking words

Look at the story about Mrs Padley on page 16.
Here are ten sentences about her. Put one of the following linking words into each gap. There are twelve linking words – two aren't used!

while/during/when/before/and/after/because/but/although/so/until/because of

1 Mrs Padley wanted a small birthday party, _____ 40 people arrived.
2 _____ her parents died, she went to live in a convent.
3 _____ her youth she saw little of the outside world.
4 She had seen very few men _____ leaving the convent.
5 She left the nuns _____ she wanted to go to London.
6 She worked as a maid _____ she first came to London.
7 She met her husband _____ she was working as an air-raid warden.
8 _____ she is 103, she still does a lot of work in the house.
9 She likes to be independent, _____ she does as much as she can for herself.
10 Friends advised her to stop gardening _____ her old age.

UNIT 4

Expressing Requests and Offers

Please and thank you

Woman Excuse me. Could you open the door for me, please?
Man Yes, of course.
Woman Thank you very much.
Man Shall I take the bags for you?
Woman No, it's all right, thank you.

Man I'm dying of thirst. Would you make me a cup of tea?
Boy OK. I'll put the kettle on.
Man And could you bring some biscuits?
Boy Yes, I'll open the new packet.

● Grammar question

In the two dialogues, underline three *requests* like this: _____
Underline three offers like this:
- - - - -

PRACTICE

Speak

Work in pairs.
You are in a hotel.
One of you is the receptionist, the other a guest.
The guest has several requests, and phones reception from her/his room.

Example
There's no hot water.

A *Hello. Reception. Can I help you?*
B *Yes. There's no hot water in my room. Could you see to it, please?*
A *Certainly. I'll send someone straight away.*

- You'd like some tea in your room.
- You want the telephone number of the railway station.
- You're expecting a Mr Smith and want to know if he's in Reception yet.
- The television doesn't work.
- You want to change some travellers' cheques.
- You'd like to be woken at 7.00 in the morning and have breakfast in your room at 7.45.
- You want to leave a message for Mr Halliday in room 301.

Listen

There are many ways of asking people to do things.
Which form we use depends who we are speaking to.

T.8 Listen to these six short dialogues.

On a separate piece of paper write down the answers to these questions.
1 Where are the people?
2 What is the relationship between them? (e.g. parent/child, customer/shop assistant)

Listen again and practise the way they ask someone to do something.

Roleplay

Work in pairs.
Prepare a dialogue together, then act it out in front of the class.
A is very busy and has lots of things to do. **B** offers to help.

Choose one of these situations.
- going on holiday (pack cases/close windows/turn off fridge/etc.)
- cooking a large meal (prepare vegetables/do the washing-up/lay table/etc.)
- your office is in chaos, the phone's ringing and an important customer is coming.

Begin like this.
A *Oh dear. There's so much to do.*
B *I'll help, if you like.*
A *That's great. Could you...?*
B *Yes, of course. Shall I...?*

A matching exercise

Match a line in column **A** with a line in column **B**.
Where are the dialogues taking place?

A Could you fill it up, please?
How would you like it?
It's a present. Could you gift-wrap it?
Two lagers, please.
Could you tell me when to get off?
Could you tell me the code for Paris?
I'll give you a lift if you like.

B Yes, I'll take the price off as well.
Just one moment. I'll look it up.
Yes, I'll give you a shout.
Shall I check the oil, too?
Halves or pints?
Would you drop me near the station?
Could I have three tens and the rest in fives?

Language review 1

Asking people to do things

Could you help me, please?
Would you open the window for me?

Could you . . .? is one of the most common forms. You can safely use it in most situations.

Translate

Could you help me, please?

_____

Would you open the window?

_____

Open your bags, please.

_____

Language review 2

Offering help

I'll help you. (I am offering to help you.)
Shall I help you? (I am asking if you would like me to help you.)

Translate

I'll open the door for you.

_____

Shall I carry your suitcase?

_____

▶ Grammar reference: page 90

SKILLS DEVELOPMENT
Vocabulary

1 Talking about nationalities.

The Italians Italian people	eat a lot of pasta.
The Russians Russian people	drink vodka.
The Greeks Greek people	are good at business.

The English English people	read a lot of newspapers.
The French French people	are good cooks.

If the adjective ends in one of these sounds   [ʃ]   [tʃ]   [s]   [z] there is no **-s** at the end.

Note: In some cases there is a word for the people that is different from the adjective.

Example
Denmark/Danish/The Danes (or *Danish people*)

2 Fill in the chart and mark the stress. Add some countries of your own. Write a sentence about the people.

Country	Adjective	A sentence about the people
'Italy	I'talian	The Italians make good cars.
Brazil		
Germany		H/W for next week (28/2/99)
Spain		
Holland		
Turkey		
Sweden		
Scotland	'Scottish (*Scotch* is whisky!)	

Reading

Pre-reading task

Work in groups.
Write as many facts and opinions about Scotland and the Scots as you can.

Compare what other members of your group have written.

Facts	Opinions
The capital is Edinburgh.	I think the weather is often bad.

Reading for gist

Read the article.
What does a mean person *not* like doing?

Comprehension check

1 What is the advertisement that the Scots don't like?
2 Who have they complained to?
3 What is the name of their organization?
4 What is the point that Mr David Webster is trying to make?
5 What is amusing in the last paragraph?

What do you think?

Do you think the Scots were right to go to the European Commission for Human Rights, or do you think they took it too seriously?

Scots in Sweden upset by cheap jokes

By Dennis Barker

1 SCOTS working in Sweden have complained to the European Commission for Human Rights that jokes about mean Scotsmen in advertising are an insult to the image of their race.

2 A case was put to Strasbourg by the Scottish Group for Civil Rights in Sweden, an organisation formed recently of Scots people working there, to protest against Swedish Railways using such a traditional joke in an advertising campaign.

3 It showed two Scotsmen accepting the offer of travel for two for the *price* of one first-class ticket, while a third hides in the luggage rack.

4 'We are not against Scots jokes in everyday life,' said Mr David Webster, a 38-year-old marketing manager working near Stockholm, who helped to form the group. 'There are nationalistic jokes like this in every country. What we don't like is the frequency of such jokes in commercial advertising.'

5 But the commission did not feel that the group had fully explained its case, and has asked for more information on some points before it decides whether the case can continue.

6 'There is even one group of cut-price shops in the Stockholm area that has changed its name to The Scot,' said Mr Webster. 'Their motto is, "You can't get it cheaper anywhere else".' These things are offensive only because they happen so often, we believe.'

7 Apart from the further information demanded by the European Commission for Human Rights, the Scots in Sweden are up against another difficulty. They have so far spent several hundred pounds on their campaign, but voluntary contributions from group members have totalled only £50.

Summarizing

Match the summary with the correct paragraph.
- [ ] a. A description of the advertisement they are complaining about.
- [ ] b. The commission's reaction.
- [ ] c. The exact reason why they are complaining.
- [ ] d. A financial problem for the Scots in Sweden.
- [ ] e. Some Scottish people have complained to the European Courts about an advertisement.
- [ ] f. Another example of their reason for complaining.
- [ ] g. They formed an organization and explained why they were complaining to the court.

Bara två kan resa så.

Är ni för gamla för tågets ungdomsrabatt (upp till 26 år)? Är ni för få för tågets familjerabatt (minst tre betalande familjemedlemmar)?

Då ska ni passa på att åka 1 klass, hela långa sommaren! Är ni två som reser tillsammans, kan ni nämligen åka 1 klass tåg verkligt billigt hela sommaren, i mån av plats. Den ene betalar fullt pris, medan den andra får hela 75% rabatt! Ni kan åka när ni vill och vart ni vill, bara ni åker minst tio mil bort och dessutom tur och retur. Bara ni är två som reser tillsammans, kan ni resa så, från och med 1 juni till och med 31 augusti. Bara två kan resa så.

Far i Par-rabatt för er två som vill resa första klass billigare.

Tåget för människor tillsammans.

Speaking

Discussion

1 Which nationalities or regional groups do people make jokes about in your country?

2 Look at this description of a stereotype. Which nationality do you think it is?

'They're overweight and loud. Their voices are loud, their behaviour is loud and their clothes are loud – yellow checked trousers and a red flowery shirt. They've always got three cameras round their neck, and they want to buy everything that's more than fifty years old.'

3 To what extent do you think there are nationality stereotypes? Are they fair? People are generally afraid of what is unfamiliar or different. Do you think this is why we have stereotype images of other nationalities?

4 What is the stereotype English man and woman? Think of their clothes, behaviour, attitudes and interests.

5 Now do the same for your nationality. What are the positive and negative qualities of the stereotype of your nationality?

These words might help you.

hard-working/lazy/ hospitable/ don't welcome foreigners
have a good sense of humour/have no sense of humour
honest
talk a lot/reserved
polite/rude
sociable
like food and drink (too much)

6 How much do you think *you* conform to this stereotype of your own nationality? How do you differ from it?

Listening

Listening for gist

Look at this picture of Mrs Gibbs, and listen to the introduction to a radio programme about her.

1 How old is she?
2 Which countries has she been to?
3 How does she travel?
4 When did she begin to travel?

T.9 Listen to the interview and take notes under these headings.

- Food and meals
- Planning where to go
- The people she meets
- The dangers of travelling
- The most beautiful place she has ever been to

Comprehension check

1 Compare your notes with another student.
Do you agree?
Listen to the tape again if necessary.
2 In what ways is Mrs Gibbs unusual for a woman of her age?
In what ways is she typical?
3 Describe an ordinary day in the life of Mrs Gibbs on her travels.

What do you think?

1 Would you like to spend your life wandering from place to place as Mrs Gibbs does?
2 Does such 'rootlessness' appeal to you or frighten you?
3 Which countries would you most like to visit?

Writing

Narrative

Here are two versions of the same story. Compare them, and decide which one you prefer, and why.

James was a student. He did not have much money.

Last year he decided to go to Manchester to visit some friends. He decided to hitchhike. He got a bus to the motorway. It was cold and he got wet. After waiting two hours he got a lift from a lorry driver, who was going to Manchester. He felt pleased. The lorry driver was a nice man, and they talked a lot. Then a police car overtook them and made them stop, and they had to go to the police station. The police thought the lorry was carrying stolen goods. A policeman asked James a lot of questions, and James spent the night in the police station. He was released the next day. The lorry was carrying stolen television sets. James said he would not hitchhike again.

James was a student at Oxford University, where he was studying law. Like many students he did not have much money because his grant was only just enough to live on. Last year, during the Autumn term, he decided to go to Manchester to visit some friends for the weekend, but he could not afford a train ticket, and even the coach was too expensive, so he had to hitchhike. He caught a bus to the beginning of the motorway and waited. It was a cold, windy November day and while he was waiting he got soaked to the skin. After waiting two hours he finally got a lift from a lorry driver, who was in fact going all the way to Manchester. James felt extremely relieved. The lorry driver seemed a friendly fellow of around 35, reasonably well-dressed, and he and James talked a lot. Suddenly, as they were driving along the motorway, a police car raced past them and made them stop. They were taken to the police station because the police suspected that the lorry was carrying stolen goods. A detective interrogated James for two hours, and he even had to spend the night in a cell. He was eventually released the next day. Apparently, the lorry was carrying stolen television sets. James swore that he would never hitchhike again.

1   What makes a good story?
    Consider the following.
    Organization
    – setting the scene
    – relating the narrative
    – concluding the story
    Description
    – people
    – places
    Language
    – vocabulary
    – the use of adjectives and
      adverbs
    – sentence construction

2   In the second story, box all the *linking devices* that join two sentences, like this for example: where .

3   Write about a memorable journey that you have made.

23

UNIT 5

Future Time – Will and Going to

Future intentions

PRESENTATION

Shopping list

sugar
tea
coffee
cheese
biscuits
cornflakes
tin of beans
yoghurt

T.10

Peter I'm just going to the shops. Do you want anything?

Anne No, I don't think so. Oh, hang on. We haven't got any sugar left.

Peter It's all right. It's on my list. I'm going to buy some.

Anne What about bread?

Peter OK. I'll go to the baker and buy a loaf.

● Grammar questions

– Why does Peter say:
I'm going to buy some (sugar); but *I'll go to the baker*.

– What's the difference between **will** and **going to** to express a future intention?

PRACTICE

1 Look at the shopping list. What else is Peter going to buy?

Example
He's going to buy some cheese.

2 Peter said *I'll go to the baker and buy a loaf.* What could he say if Anne said she wanted the things in the pictures? Which shops would Peter go to?

Example
Anne *Could you get some stamps?*
Peter *OK. I'll go to the Post Office and buy some stamps.*

Anne wants these things.

Pairwork

It's Christmas, and time to buy presents for everyone.

Student A You have already decided what you are going to buy for everyone.

Student B You are looking for suggestions.

B What are you going to buy for Henry?

A A record.

B What shall I buy him? What does he like doing?

A He likes reading.

B Right. I'll buy him a book.

Do the same for these people.

Anne – likes gardening
John – likes painting
James – likes cooking
Aunt Sally – likes making wine
Uncle Bob – likes model railways
Kate (aged 3) – likes playing with dolls

Now do the same for the members of your class!

24

Listen

T.11 Listen to this weather forecast for the British Isles, and put the symbols in the correct place on the map.

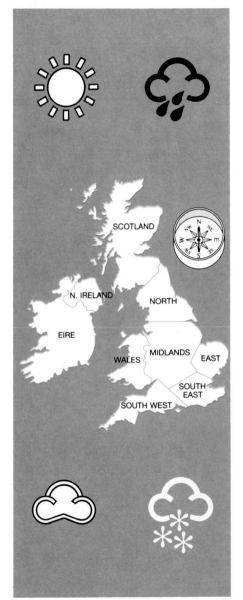

What is today's weather forecast where you are?

Language review 1

Will: Uses

We use **will**:

1 To make a future prediction. (This can be a personal opinion.)
*I think it **will** rain tomorrow.*

2 To talk about a future fact.
*The Queen **will** open the new hospital on Thursday.*
*He'**ll** be 45 next week.*

3 To express a future intention or decision, often one made at the moment of speaking.
  A *Did you know John's in hospital?*
  B *No, I didn't. **I'll** go and visit him this afternoon.*

Sat · 11.00 6th March

Translate

It will rain tomorrow.

It won't snow.

A Can I ring you this evening?
B Yes. I'll give you my number. 40983.

Waiter What would you like to eat?
Customer I'll have a steak, please.

◀ **Look back** at page 24 and underline the examples of **will**.

Language review 2

Going to: Use

We use **going to** to express a future intention, plan or decision thought about before the moment of speaking.

*When we go to France, we're **going to** stay in a hotel.*
(It's already booked.)

Translate

We're going to stay in a hotel.

He isn't going to do any work.

What are you going to do in America?

◀ **Look back** at page 24 and underline the examples of **going to**.

▶ **Grammar reference:** page 91.

SKILLS DEVELOPMENT
Speaking

Roleplay

In pairs, prepare a conversation according to these instructions.

Students A phones **Student B**

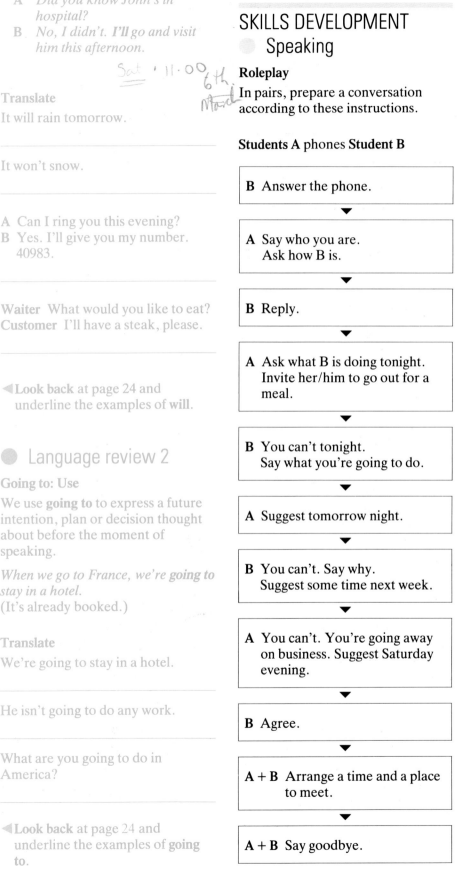

I am always both amused and annoyed when I hear foreign people criticize English food. 'It's unimaginative,' they say. 'It's boring, it's tasteless, it's chips with everything and totally overcooked vegetables.' 'It's unambitious,' say the French, 'all you do is roasts with jam.' (We eat apple sauce with pork.) That's the bit they find really shocking, but then the French are easily shocked by things that aren't French.

When I ask these visitors where they have experienced English cooking, I am astonished by their reply. 'In Wimpy Bars and MacDonald's Hamburger restaurants,' they often say. I have won my case. Their conclusions are inexcusable.

I have a theory about English cooking, and I was interested to read that several famous cookery writers agree with me. My theory is this. Our basic ingredients, when fresh, are so full of flavour that we haven't had to invent sauces and complex recipes to disguise their natural taste. What can compare with fresh peas or new potatoes just boiled (not overboiled) and served with butter? Why drown spring lamb in wine or cream or yoghurt and spices, when with just one or two herbs it is absolutely delicious?

It is interesting to speculate what part

Illustration: Traditional English roast for Sunday lunch.

factors such as geography and climate play in the creation of a country's food. We complain about our wet and changeable weather, but it is the rain which gives us our rich soil and green grass. 'Abroad,' says Jane Grigson, 'poor soils meant more searching for food, more discovery, more invention, whereas our ancestors sat down to plenty without having to take trouble.'

If you ask foreigners to name some typically English dishes, they will probably say 'Fish and chips' and then stop. It is disappointing, but true, that there is no tradition in England of eating in restaurants, because our food doesn't lend itself to such preparation. English cooking is found in the home, where it is possible to time the dishes to perfection. So it is difficult to find a good English restaurant with reasonable prices.

It is for these reasons that we haven't exported our dishes, but we have imported a surprising number from all over the world. In most cities in Britain you'll find Indian, Chinese, French and Italian restaurants. In London you'll also find Indonesian, Lebanese, Iranian, German, Spanish, Mexican, Greek . . . Cynics will say that this is because we have no 'cuisine' ourselves, but, well, you know what I think!

Reading

What do you think influences a country's food?

Reading for gist

Read this magazine article about English food.

Comprehension check

1 Which of these titles do you think is best?
– Fish and Chips against the world!
– Cosmopolitan English cooking
– In defence of English cooking
– Fresh is best in the English kitchen
– English Food: Facts or Myth?
2 What is the author's main point about English food?
3 Why doesn't he agree with foreign people's criticism of English food?
4 What is the comparison that Jane Grigson makes?
5 Why are there few English restaurants?

What do you think?

1 What kind of person wrote this article? What makes you think so?
2 Who do you think Jane Grigson is?
3 'I have won my case.' (Line 23) What is meant by this?
4 Do you agree with this article? Read it again and mark it like this.
   I agree   ✓
   I don't agree   X
   I find this surprising   !!
   I don't understand this   ?

   Summarize each paragraph in one or two sentences.

Vocabulary

Word formation: adjectives ending with -ing and -ed

Look at lines 9 and 10 of the article. What's the difference between **shocking** and **shocked**?

Which	describes the person's reaction? is passive?

Which	describes the action? is active?

Some verbs which describe people's feelings have two adjectival forms.

Example

to shock/shock**ed**/*I was shocked by the news.*
to shock/shock**ing**/*The news was shocking.*

1 Find other words like this in the article. Sometimes only one of the two is there, but you can write both in the columns.
Note: These are only words that tell us about people's *feelings* (not words like 'cooking').

Adjectives ending in -ed
amused

Adjectives ending in -ing
amusing

Can you add any more to the list?

2 Put one suitable adjective (**-ed** or **-ing**) into each gap.
a. The book was so _____ that I couldn't put it down.
b. The students were _____ by the lesson and nearly fell asleep.
c. John told some very _____ stories. We couldn't stop laughing.
d. **A** You look _____ to see me!
   B I am. I thought you were in China!
e. She's very _____ in modern art. She reads all the books she can about it.
f. Your exam results are _____. I thought you would do much better.
g. Please stop tapping your fingers. I find it very _____.

3 What do you think of . . .?

westerns/horror films/modern architecture/the latest fashions/ political programmes on television/opera/this book/ children

Dictionary work

The following words are in the text. Use your dictionary to find the other parts of speech. Check the pronunciation.

noun	adjective	verb
creation		
	basic	
conclusion		

noun	verb
	to agree
	to invent
	to complain
discovery	
preparation	

noun	adjective
	famous
theory	
tradition	
	possible

Pre-listening task

Are these statements about China true (T) or false (F)?

a. It has a population of more than one thousand million.
b. It is the largest country in the world.
c. There are records of what was happening in China nearly four thousand years ago.
d. It has been a Socialist Republic since 1949.
e. It does not want links with the rest of the world.
f. Tourists can travel freely in China.
g. English is commonly spoken in China.

Listening for specific information

T.12   Listen to this phone-in radio programme about China. Answer the true/false questions.

Comprehension check/Language work

1 What is the first caller going to do soon?
2 What does Kate Leigh tell him about the kind of life he will have?
3 What do the Chinese like doing in the evening?
4 What does China want from the rest of the world?
5 What, according to Dr Scott, are the two things China is trying to do?
6 What sort of a holiday will the third caller have?
7 How does Kate Leigh describe the Chinese?

What do you think?

1 Would you like to visit China?
2 Look at question 5 above. Do you think China will be able to do these things?
3 What sort of dishes is Chinese cooking famous for?
4 There were several other questions from callers. Can you answer these questions?
   What is the climate like?
   Is the Chinese language easy to learn?

Is Chinese medicine as advanced as the West's?
What is China doing to control its population?
5 What questions would you like to ask about China?

The date can also be written
March 4th 1985, or 4/3/85. First
the date, then the month, then the
year.

If you don't know the person's
name, begin the letter, 'Dear Sir,'
or 'Dear Sir or Madam,'
Notice the comma.

The name and address of the
people you're writing to.

Your address, but *not* your name.

```
                                              17, Brick Street,
                                              London.  S.W.1.

                                              4th March 1985

         Breakaway,
         84, Clarendon Road,
         Colchester.

         Dear Sir,

         I saw your advertisement for holiday cottages in the
         Guardian newspaper.

         Could you please send me a copy of your 1985 brochure,
         and include information such as price lists and booking
         arrangements?

         I look forward to hearing from you, and thank you in
         advance.

         Yours faithfully,

         John Naunton

         John Naunton
```

You can indent or begin on the
left-hand side. It doesn't matter.
But keep to one style in one letter.

Writing

A formal letter of enquiry

1 Notice the organization of the letter.
– **Paragraph 1** Introduction.
– **Paragraph 2** The body of the letter.
– **Paragraph 3** The conclusion.
– **Ending** 'Yours faithfully,' if you begin 'Dear Sir,' and 'Yours sincerely,' if you begin 'Dear Mr Smith,'.
– **Your signature** and your name printed clearly underneath.

2 Notice that most letters in English, formal and informal, begin with 'Dear . . .,'
If you don't know the name of the person you're writing to, begin *Dear Sir*, or *Dear Sir or Madam*,

If you know the name of the person you're writing to, begin *Dear Mr Brown*, *Dear Mrs Black*, *Dear Miss Jones*, *Dear Ms Jackson*,

It is becoming more frequent to address women as *Ms* in business letters, whether you know they are married or not.

3 Some useful phrases
a. Asking someone to do something
Could you please . . .? (Not *Please could you . . .*)
I would be (most) grateful if you could . . .
b. Saying you have included another document
Please find enclosed a cheque for . . .
I enclose a stamped addressed envelope.
c. Ending the letter
I look forward to hearing from you soon.
(*I look* is formal; *I'm looking* is informal.)
I hope to hear from you soon is slightly more informal.

4 There are no contractions in a formal letter.

I have	not	I've
I am		I'm

Write a letter in reply to this advertisement, which you saw in a magazine called *Today*.

You also want to know about accommodation and the cost of living in London.

Is there any other information you would like?

UNIT 6

Describing People and Places

Asking for descriptions

PRESENTATION

T.13

Man Where are you going for your holidays this year? Have you decided?

Woman Yes, we're going to Corsica.

Man Oh. I know Corsica well. I spent a year there.

Woman Really? What's it like?

Man It's very beautiful. It's got everything. Mountains, beaches, and good weather.

Woman And what are the people like?

Man They're quite independent, but when you get to know them, they're very friendly. You'll have a really good time.

1 Does the man describe Corsica generally or in detail?
2 Does the man describe the Corsicans' appearance or character?

Paul Anna, what was your first boyfriend like?

Anna Goodness! Why do you want to know that?

Paul I'm just interested.

Anna Well, he was very good-looking, with dark hair and big, brown eyes. He was very romantic. He was always buying me flowers and presents. Of course, he wasn't as nice as you.

1 What do you think Paul wants to know about her first boyfriend? About his appearance, his character, or both?
2 Does Anna tell him about her boyfriend's appearance, or character, or both?

Old Lady Help me somebody please! Oh policeman, stop that man!

Policeman I . . .

Old Lady He stole my handbag!

Policeman I think it's too late, madam.

Old Lady But . . .

Policeman He's escaped.

Old Lady Mm . . .

Policeman Now tell me . . .

Old Lady Yes . . .

Policeman What did he look like?

Old Lady Ah well . . . He . . . He was medium height and err . . . quite . . . er . . . well built and he had short dark hair. Oh I know he looked like that actor man, that David Starr. You know um . . . the actor, well yes he did but he was taller than that.

● Grammar question

There are four questions on this page that ask for descriptions. Underline them. What is the difference between:
What is he like?
What does he look like?

PRACTICE

1 Talk in pairs and quickly find a country or a town that one of you knows but the other doesn't.

Student A You have been to *X*.
Student B You haven't been to *X*.

First prepare on your own.

Student A You are going to describe this place. Think of the location/size/people/weather, etc.

Student B You are going to ask questions to find out about this place. What do you want to know about the climate?/the restaurants?/the nightlife?

Ask questions like this:
What is . . . like?
What are . . . like?

Now talk together.

2 Look at these questions.
a. What does she like?
b. What is she like?
c. What does she look like?
d. How is she?

They are similar in form but they are not the same in meaning. Say which answer (1, 2, 3, 4) goes with each question (a, b, c, d), and discuss the differences between the questions.

1 She's not very well, actually. She's got a bad cold.
2 She's really nice. Very friendly and open, and good fun to be with.
3 She likes swimming and skiing, and she's a keen football fan.
4 She's quite tall, average build, with straight brown hair.

3 **T.14** You're going to hear ten short tapes. Each one is the answer to one of the questions under 2 (a, b, c or d). Listen to the tapes and decide which is the most appropriate question. Write your answer here. The first one is done for you.

1 [b] 2 [d] 3 [a] 4 [b] 5 [c]
6 [d] 7 [c] 8 [b] 9 [a] 10 [d]

Comparatives and superlatives

PRESENTATION

HOUSES & FLATS FOR SALE

ESTATE AGENTS

LOCATION	City centre
PRICE	£45,000
BEDROOMS	1 large 1 small
RECEPTION ROOMS	A living room with space for a table
KITCHEN	Small
GARDEN	No
SHOPS	Very close
TIME TO GET TO THE CENTRE	2 minutes
DESCRIPTION	Flat in a central position, very convenient for shops and entertainment. Modern and clean.

31

```
LOCATION            Suburbs

PRICE               £52,000

BEDROOMS            3 good size

RECEPTION ROOMS     Living room and separate dining room

KITCHEN             Small

GARDEN              Small

SHOPS               5 minutes away

TIME TO GET TO      30 minutes
THE CENTRE

DESCRIPTION         Semi-detached house in a leafy suburb.  Quiet
                    residential street close to schools and park.
                    Best of both worlds.
```

```
LOCATION            The country

PRICE               £55,000

BEDROOMS            1 very big
                    2 small

RECEPTION ROOMS     Large living room and small dining room

KITCHEN             Very large

GARDEN              Big

SHOPS               15 minutes away

TIME TO GET TO      50 minutes
THE CENTRE

DESCRIPTION         A country cottage - everyone's dream.  Peace
                    and quiet away from the rest of the world.
                    Completely isolated.
```

PRACTICE

Pairwork

1 Where would you like to live?
2 Why?

Group work

Try to persuade those who disagree with you that your choice is best.

Example
A *I'd like to live in the flat because it's nearest to the centre.*
B *But it's smaller than the others and much noisier. I'd like . . .*

A class questionnaire

Talk to all the students in your language class. Find the answers to these questions:
1 Who lives nearest to school?
2 Who has the longest journey to school?
3 Who lives furthest from the shops?
4 Who has the biggest garden?

First decide what questions you are going to ask everyone. These questions will help you:
Where . . .?   How far . . .?
How long . . .?   How big . . .?

● Language review 1

Asking for descriptions

1 *What's London like?* means: 'Describe London to me because I don't know anything about it.' It is a very general question. When it is asked about a person, the answer can refer either to character or to appearance or both.

   What's John like?
   1 *He's very friendly.*
   2 *He's good looking.*
   3 *He's quite nice, but he isn't very handsome.*

2 *What does she look like?* asks for a description of her physical appearance, not her character.
   A *What does she look like?*
   B *She's tall, and she's got blue eyes and blonde hair.*

3 *How are your parents?* asks about their health and general happiness only. It does not ask for a description.
   A *How are your parents?*
   B *They're fine, thanks. My mother had a cold but she's better now.*

Translate

What's London like?

What does she look like?

How are your parents?

◄Look back at page 31 and underline the examples of these questions.

● Language review 2

Comparatives and Superlatives

Adjectives and adverbs have a **comparative** and **superlative** form.
Japanese is easier to learn than English.
You must do your homework more carefully.

It was the most difficult decision I ever had to make.

Remember also:
as . . . as expresses equality
not as/so . . . as expresses inequality.
Dogs are as stupid as cats, but they're not as/so clean.

Translate
I am younger than you.

I am the youngest in my family.

Do your homework more carefully.

Buses aren't as fast as trains.

◀ **Look back** at page 32 and underline the examples of **comparatives** and **superlatives**.

▶ Grammar reference: page 92.

SKILLS DEVELOPMENT
Vocabulary

Vocabulary of character: What sort of person are you?

1 Put Y for Yes, N for No, and S for Sometimes
a. ☐ Are you generally aware of other people's feelings?
b. ☐ Do you find it difficult to meet new people?
c. ☐ Do you frequently make people laugh?
d. ☐ Does your mood change often and suddenly?
e. ☐ When decisions have to be made, do you think first of yourself?
f. ☐ Can your friends trust you and depend on you?
g. ☐ Do you generally like other people's company?
h. ☐ Are there lots of things you want to do in your professional life?
i. ☐ Can you usually understand other people's point of view?

j. ☐ Do you worry and think too much about detail?
k. ☐ Are you usually quite a happy, smiling person?
l. ☐ Are you interested in other people and their business?
m.☐ Do you sometimes not tell the truth because you don't want to hurt someone's feelings?

2 Match these adjectives with the questions above.

Example **b** shy

☐ tolerant   ☐ witty
☐ sociable   ☐ selfish
☐ reliable   ☐ ambitious
☐ sensitive   ☐ moody
☐ tactful   ☐ inquisitive
☐ fussy   ☐ cheerful

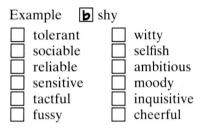

3 Which of these do you think are *positive*, and which *negative* qualities?

4 What are the opposites of these adjectives?

Sometimes you can form the opposite using a **prefix** or **suffix**.
Prefixes: in-/un-
Suffix: -less

Sometimes one word doesn't describe the idea. You will need to think of a sentence like:
He/She's the kind of person who . . .

5 ☐ **T.15** ☐ Listen to these people describing someone.
Who do you think they are describing? A relative? Someone they know professionally?

33

Reading

1 Work in groups. First every member of the group makes two lists.
a. What are the advantages of growing old?
b. What are the disadvantages? Think of: health/experience/family/work

Now discuss your lists with each other and prepare one complete list for the group.

2 What do you understand by these sayings?
You can't teach an old dog new tricks.
There's no fool like an old fool.

Read this poem.

Warning

T.16　When I am an old woman I shall wear purple
With a red hat which doesn't go, and doesn't suit me,
And I shall spend my pension on brandy and summer gloves
And satin sandals, and say we've no money for butter.
I shall sit down on the pavement when I'm tired
And gobble up samples in shops and press alarm bells
And run my stick along the public railings
And make up for the sobriety of my youth.
I shall go out in my slippers in the rain
And pick the flowers in other people's gardens
And learn to spit.

You can wear terrible shirts and grow more fat
And eat three pounds of sausages at a go
Or only bread and pickle for a week
And hoard pens and pencils and beermats and things in boxes.

But now we must have clothes that keep us dry
And pay our rent and not swear in the street
And set a good example for the children.
We will have friends to dinner and read the papers.

But maybe I ought to practise a little now?
So people who know me are not too shocked and surprised
When suddenly I am old and start to wear purple.

Jenny Joseph

Check any words you don't know.

What do you think?

1 What do you understand by the title of the poem? Who is she warning?
2 The poem has three parts. Where do you think the divisions are?
3 Which part(s) of the poem refer to:
– the distant future?
– the near future?
– the present?
– the past?
4 What sort of things is she going to do when she is an old woman? Why can't she do them now?
5 Who is *you* in verse 2?
6 Use your imagination to describe the woman and the life she leads now.
– How old is she?
– How many children has she got?
– Has she got a job?
– What social class does she belong to?
– Is she happy?
– What sort of clothes does she wear?

What she wants to do in the future contrasts with what she does now, so read the first three verses again.

Speaking

Discussion

Normally we like to surround ourselves with people of the same interests and opinions. This is how groups are formed.

1 What has brought these groups of people together?
– a trade union
– a football crowd
– the Hollywood Oscar ceremony
– freemasons
– scouts and guides
– members of a golf or tennis club
– prisoners
– members of anti-nuclear groups
– nuns
– members of the armed forces
– royalty

2 Choose some of the groups and describe for each one
a. what is normal, acceptable behaviour for this group.
b. some examples of what would be unacceptable to the other members of the group.

3 To how many of these groups can you attach a certain social class?

Example
People who belong to trade unions are traditionally working class, but many of them are also middle class.

4 How much of a class system is there in your country? How does it show itself? Is there an aristocracy?

Listening

T.17 Divide into two groups. Each group is going to listen to a different tape.

On tape (A) an English husband and wife, Bob and Sheila, talk about the time they lived in New York.
On tape (B), Terry talks about her impressions of living and working in England.

While you are listening to your tape, take notes under these headings.
– Their general impressions of the country
– The people
– Shops
– Life styles

When you have listened, pair up with a member of the other group, and compare notes.

Writing

Set out and punctuate the following formal letter correctly.
Divide it into paragraphs if you think it is necessary.

13 chesnut st durham 17 march 1985 globe furniture 166 henly st london w1 dear mr bradburn i recently ordered from you a set of four french dining room chairs and an italian coffee table both of which were advertised in the january edition of home and gardens magazine they arrived as promised but unfortunately they were damaged the coffee table had one of its legs broken and the backs of the chairs were scratched i understand these items are under guarantee could you please tell me what i should do look forward to hearing from you yours sincerely james p robinson

Present Perfect Simple

A job interview

PRESENTATION

SALES DIRECTOR

Anglo-Tours is an expanding company that has been in operation for over 10 years.

Applicants for the post of Sales Director should be aged between 35–50, and have considerable experience in sales and marketing, in the UK and abroad.

Salary £20,000 plus.

Write, giving details of background and experience, to

**Personnel Manager,
Anglo-Tours,
232 Bristol Road,
Ashford.**

T.18 John Wigmore is being interviewed by Harriet Brown, the Managing Director of a tour company. Mr Wigmore has applied for the post of Sales Director.

Ms Brown Who do you work for now, Mr Wigmore?

Mr Wigmore The National Bus Company.

Ms Brown And how long have you worked for them?

Mr Wigmore I've worked for them for five years.

Ms Brown How long have you been an area sales manager?

Mr Wigmore Eighteen months.

Ms Brown And what did you do before joining the Bus Company?

Mr Wigmore I worked for a chain of hotels as junior manager.

● Grammar questions

Explain why Mr Wigmore says:
I've worked for (the Bus Company) for five years. But *I worked for a chain of hotels.*

– Is he still area sales manager for the Bus Company?
– Does he still work for a chain of hotels?

Ms Brown The post you've applied for involves a lot of travelling. Have you been abroad much?

Mr Wigmore I've been to most of western Europe, and I've been to central Europe once, to Hungary.

Ms Brown Why did you go there?

Mr Wigmore The hotel sent me to attend a conference.

Ms Brown I see. Have you ever organized a conference yourself?

Mr Wigmore Yes, I have actually. Why?

Ms Brown Well, this job would require rather a lot of organizing meetings and conferences.

● Grammar questions

Ms Brown asks:
*Have you been abroad much?
Have you ever organized a conference yourself?*

– Is she interested in exactly *when* he did these things?
– Or is she asking about his experience, *some time* in his life?
– If Ms Brown wanted to know *when* Mr Wigmore went to Hungary and *when* he organized a conference, what would her questions be?

When . . .?

PRACTICE

Answer these questions about yourself:

How long have you known your teacher?

_____

How long have you lived at your present address?

_____

When did you move there?

_____

How long have you had your present job?

_____

What did you do before that?

_____

Now ask your partner the same questions.

Pairwork

Make up dialogues like this.

see/Shakespeare play?
A *Have you ever seen a Shakespeare play?*
B *Yes, I have./No, I haven't.*
A *When did you see it?*
B *Two years ago. I saw 'Hamlet'.*

try/Indian food?
have/car accident?
ride/a horse?
work/factory?
have/operation?
meet/someone famous?
be/United States? (Careful)
write/any poetry?
win/any money?
have/your name in the newspapers?

Giving news of recent events

PRESENTATION

T.19   You are going to hear the radio news.
First you will hear the headlines, then the whole stories.
Fill in the gaps.

Headlines

An American airliner _____, killing all 178 people on board.
The lorry drivers' strike _____ after two days of negotiations between management and the unions.
England's boxing champion, Tony Fellows, ____ in Mexico.

Stories

Last night a Pan-Am Boeing 747 _____ just ten miles from the Irish coast.
The lorry drivers' strike _____ as drivers accepted a new pay deal which will give them a rise of £10 per week.
_____, Tony Fellows, _____ in Mexico City. His opponent knocked him out in the eighth round.

Grammar questions

Two different tenses are used in the headline and the story.
– What are they?
– What is the difference?

PRACTICE

What's in the news at the moment?
Write the headline and a short story for something that has happened recently
– in the world
– in your country
– in your town

The Present Perfect

The *Present Perfect* relates past actions and states to the present.

It is used:
1 To express **unfinished past**:
I've been in my present job for six years.
I've lived here all my life.

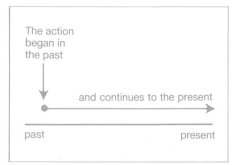

The action began in the past

and continues to the present

past   present

2 To express **experience**:
Have you ever been to Australia?
I've had two crashes in my career as a racing driver.

The action happened in the past,
but we don't know when
or we're not interested in when

● ?   ● ?

past   present

1960?   1974?   1980?

s o m e   t i m e   i n   y o u r   l i f e .

3 To express the **present result** of a past event:
I've lost my wallet. Have you seen it?
She's broken her leg, so she can't play tennis.

The action happened in the past, usually the recent past

with results in the present.

past   present

Translate

I live in London

I've lived here for ten years.

I lived in Rome before I came here.

He has never seen a Shakespeare play.

She saw 'Hamlet' yesterday.

I've lost my wallet.

I lost it last night.

◀ **Look back** at pages 37 and 38 and underline the examples of the *Present Perfect*. Which uses are they?

▶ Grammar reference: page 93.

SKILLS DEVELOPMENT
● Reading

Arranging jumbled texts

Here are three stories about people who have started their own businesses, but the stories have been mixed up.
First read the paragraphs quickly and decide which paragraphs go with which story.
Then put them in the right order.

James McClarty:
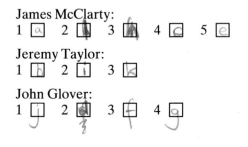
1 [a] 2 [l] 3 [f] 4 [c] 5 [e]

Jeremy Taylor:
1 [b] 2 [i] 3 [k]

John Glover:
1 [j] 2 [d] 3 [f] 4 [g]

---

a.

James McClarty, 16, runs a part-time bakery delivery service. Every Friday evening he goes round his local village selling his wares—bread, rolls and teacakes, which he buys wholesale from a bakery.

b.

Jeremy Taylor has had his market garden for 18 months now, growing fruit and vegetables for local consumption. He is most proud of his early potatoes and juicy raspberries. He thought starting a business would be complicated, but in fact he found it was quite straightforward.

c.

He had the excellent idea of giving out free hot cross buns before Easter, and as a result he got bumper orders for the Easter weekend. 'I've already expanded to include the next village, but I've employed a friend to do the delivering.'

d.

But there weren't any. 'I still had £100 and my bike. I'm lousy at mathematics, but my girlfriend Lynn was good at accounts, so we set up with another friend, Paul, as a third partner.'

e.

James likes the extra money, but he does have one complaint. 'I'm getting fat. I can't help eating the teacakes!'

f.

At first they found it very difficult to get known. 'Nothing seemed to work—leaflets and adverts in the paper brought nobody.' Then slowly the customers trickled in.

g.

Since then they have grown and grown. 'We use up to 20 riders and we buy ourselves a new bike every year. We've learned a lot about management, and we're now pretty confident about the future.'

h.

But his organization is far from old-fashioned. He has bought a computer, which he uses to work out orders, costs and profit. He has had the business for nine months.

i.

He was given good advice by his bank manager. 'Start small, consolidate and expand gradually. There's been an increased demand for really fresh vegetables, and my produce is picked, packed and sold within 24 hours.'

j.

A clever observation by John Glover gave him and two of his friends the idea for their small business. 'We'd all had jobs but we were made redundant. I had seen a lot of motorcycle couriers in London, so I thought I would try and get a job with one locally.'

k.

'I've always loved gardening, and the thought of making a living out of a hobby is wonderful.'

l.

'There hasn't been a baker in the village since the big supermarkets opened in town 10 years ago. People like the service and especially the old-fashioned bread.'

Comprehension check

1 Give each article a title.
Give an overall title for the three articles.

2 Which of the businesses
– employs the most people?
– is the smallest?
– is most affected by bad weather?
– is expanding most quickly?
– is based in a town?
– is not only a job but a hobby?
– gave away free gifts to attract customers?

Language work

1 Look again at the story about James McClarty.
In groups discuss why you put the paragraphs in a certain order.

2 There are many examples of the *Present Perfect* in the stories.
Underline some, and discuss why the *Present Perfect* was used.

3 Here are the answers to some questions.
Work out the questions.

James McClarty
a. Once a week.
b. From a bakery.
c. 10 years ago.
d. A computer.
e. Nine months.
f. Yes. His business now includes deliveries to the next village.

John Glover
a. In London.
b. Three.
c. They printed leaflets and advertised in the paper.

Vocabulary

Guessing the meaning of unknown words

When you read you don't always want to stop to look up a word you don't understand in a dictionary. If it's not important read on. But you can often guess the meaning of the word.

What do you think is the meaning of the words in italics?
1 I can't use this knife. It's too *blunt*.

2 In my bedroom there's a table, a chair, a bed and a *wardrobe*.
3 His clothes were *spotless*, but his face was dirty.

How sure are you that you *know* the meaning? 90%? 50%? 100%? What were the clues that helped you?

Try to work out the meaning of these words.
Paragraph A
part-time/rolls/teacakes/ buys wholesale
Paragraph C
hot cross buns/bumper orders/ expanded
Paragraph E
can't help eating
Paragraph B
juicy/straightforward
Paragraph I
consolidate/expand gradually/ picked, packed and sold
Paragraph J
made redundant/locally
Paragraph D
lousy at mathematics
Paragraph F
leaflets/trickled in

Speaking

Roleplay: Getting a bank loan

Student A You want to borrow £25,000 to start a small business. Decide what the business is:
– A hotel?
– A factory?
– Import/export?

Prepare to explain to the bank manager:
– your business experience
 (*I've worked as a . . ./for . . .*)
– your experience in the business you want to start
– the preparation you've already done
 (*I've found . . ./asked . . ./ started . . .*)
– what the competition is
– how much capital you already have
– what exactly you want to do with the loan
– how soon you can pay it back

Student B You are a bank manager. Student A is going to ask you for a loan of £25,000 to start a small business.
Prepare the questions you want to ask her/him about:

– business experience
 Where have you worked . . .?
 What experience have you got . . .?
– what preparation has been done
 Have you found an office?
 Have you done any market research?
– the competitors
– the capital that he/she already has
– why he/she wants the loan
– the problems involved
 Have you thought of . . .?

How soon do you want the loan repaid?
Can you decide whether to give the loan at the end of the interview or do you need more time?

Listening

T.20 Here is an interview with Harold Thomas, who after 40 years of a full working life and 30 years as managing director of his own company, is now retired.
Listen to the interview and answer the questions.

Comprehension check/Language work

1 What are some of the things he has started doing since his retirement?
He's . . .
2 What does he particularly like about the golf club?
3 Why is he brown?
4 Which countries has he been to?
5 Which of these questions is correct?
– How long was he retired?
– How long has he been retired?
– How long is he retired?
– How long was he married?
– How long has he been married?
– How long is he married?
6 What's the answer to these questions?
7 When did he begin to get in touch with his relatives?

What do you think?

1 Do you agree with Harold Thomas that work gives direction and discipline to one's life?
If you disagree, say *why*.
2 What do you look forward to doing when you have retired?
Or would you prefer to carry on working?

Writing

Informal letters

Compare the lay-out of this informal letter with the formal letter on page 29. In what ways is it similar, and in what ways different?

Think of:
– the address
– the date
– the salutation
– the organization of the letter: introduction/body/conclusion

1 What is the main reason for this letter?
– to apologize?
– to invite?
– to accept an invitation?
– to give news?

Underline with a solid line
_____ the part of the letter that is the main reason for writing.

2 An informal letter can sound like spoken English
Underline with a broken line
_ _ _ _ _ the parts that sound like someone speaking rather than writing.

3 Box like this [ ] the verbs in the *Past Simple* that give news.

4 Circle like this ◯ the verbs that give *future plans*.

5 There are several ways of ending an informal letter.
With love,/Best wishes,/Regards,

6 Some useful phrases:
a. Beginning the letter
It was lovely to hear from you. I was pleased to hear that . . .
Thank you for your letter. I was sorry to hear that . . .
I'm sorry I haven't written before, but . . .
This is just a note to say . . .
b. Giving general news
I'm having a lovely time in . . .

I'm . . .
I've been very busy recently. Last week I . . . and next week I'm going to . . .
c. Ending the letter
I'm looking forward to seeing you . . ./to hearing from you . . .
('*I'm looking*' is informal; '*I look*' is formal)
Give my regards to your mother.
Write to me soon.
I hope to hear from you soon.
Write and tell me when you . . ./ where you . . .

7 There are contractions in an informal letter:
I'll/I'd/I'm/He's/She's/We've/etc.

Now write a letter to a friend accepting an invitation to a party. Give details of your travel arrangements (you're arriving by train) and ask if you can stay the night. Give some of your news.

H/W 9.4.99

14, Arol Road.
London N.W.6.

12th Feb, 1986

Dear Jane,

Thank you for your letter. It was lovely to hear from you, and yes, I'd really like to come and stay next weekend. You know how much I love spending weekends in the country after working all week in the city. I'll catch the usual train on Friday evening.

Do you remember Harry? well, I met him at a party the other day. He's fine, busy as always. we went to the theatre together and saw an amusing play by Stoppard.

Anyway, I'll give you more of my news when I see you. Must rush now because I'm going to see Jack's new flat this evening. I'm really looking forward to the weekend. Give my best wishes to Peter and the children.

Love, Pat

UNIT 8

Expressing Obligation

Hotel rules

PRESENTATION

Some hotels have a lot of rules!

ALL GUESTS MUST SIGN THE REGISTER IMMEDIATELY ON ARRIVAL

The Management

Guests <u>must not</u> use any electrical appliances in their room (shavers excepted) without the permission of the Management.

Guests should not leave valuables in their bedrooms. The Management cannot be held responsible for loss or theft.

● Grammar question

Underline the words that express *obligation*.
What is the difference between them?

PRACTICE

How does the receptionist express the rules in column **A**?

Use:
should/shouldn't/have to/mustn't and match them with a line in column **B**.

Example
You mustn't make any noise after 11.00 or you'll wake the other guests.

A
- make any noise after 11.00
- give me your valuables
- settle your account tonight
- take a seat in the dining room early
- smoke in bed
- pay cash for drinks
- arrive back late
- have guests in your bedroom
- produce a cheque card
- lock your room at night

B
- if you're leaving before breakfast.
- because it gets full very quickly.
- because we've had a few thefts.
- I'm afraid I can't put them on your bill.
- or you'll wake the other guests.
- and I'll put them in the safe.
- They must be entertained in the lounge.
- because you could cause a fire.
- if you want to pay by cheque.
- because the front door's locked at midnight.

Pairwork

Make up dialogues in these situations.
Student A You have just been offered a job as a tourist guide in your town.
Ask your employer about your duties, hours of work, breaks, etc.
Student B You have employed Student A to be a tourist guide. Tell her/him about the duties of the job.

St Michael ®

lily
ORIENTAL HYBRID

Student A You have just bought an exotic plant and want to know how to look after it. Ask about feeding, watering, where to put it etc.
Student B You are an expert on exotic plants. Give Student A advice on how to look after her/his plant.

Listen

> **T.21** Angela saw this advertisement for a room to let, and decided to phone to ask for more information.

```
ROOM TO LET

Family house

Convenient for public
transport

Would suit student

Reasonable rent

Phone 678 5423 -
any time
```

These are the things she wanted to ask the landlord about.
- rent
- bathroom and kitchen
- single or shared room
- house rules, visitors, hours
- how far to public transport
Do you think the accommodation and rules sound reasonable?

● Language review

Expressing obligation

Obligation is expressed by **must**, **should** and **have to**.

1 Strong obligation

*You **must** do this exercise again.*
*Hotel guests **must** sign the register.* (A notice)
*You **have to** sign your name here.* (The receptionist explains to a guest.)
*You **mustn't** smoke in bed.* (Prohibition, i.e. an obligation *not* to do something.)

Must expresses the authority of the speaker.
Have to refers to obligation in general.

2 Mild obligation/suggestion

*You **should** go to bed earlier if you feel tired.* (suggestion)
*You **should** apologize to him.* (mild obligation)
*You **shouldn't** read until 3.00 in the morning.* (suggestion)

3 Past obligation

Must does not have a past tense form.
We use **had to** to express past obligation.
*We **had to** leave early to catch the plane.*

4 Asking about obligation

Must is rarely found in the question form.

We normally use **have to** to ask about obligation.
*Do I **have to** wear a uniform?*
*What time do you **have to** get up?*

5 No obligation

*You **don't have to** iron nylon shirts.*

Translate

Passengers must have a valid ticket.

He has to work hard to pay the bills.

You mustn't steal.

You should go to the doctor.

You shouldn't smoke.

Millionaires don't have to work.

◀ **Look back** at page 42 and underline the verbs that express *obligation*.

▶ **Grammar reference:** page 94.

SKILLS DEVELOPMENT
● Reading

Written language is organized into paragraphs. Most paragraphs have a key sentence that summarizes the content of the whole paragraph. This is called the *topic sentence*. It is usually the first sentence in the paragraph, but not always. If you read the topic sentences only, you can often predict the rest.

On the next page there is an article from a family magazine. Here are the title, the picture that appeared with it, and the first sentence of the first nine paragraphs.

RUN YOUR WAY TO HEALTH
Whether you want to jog gently round the park or to train for a marathon, start running now. Oliver Gillie is convinced you'll feel better for i

When I started running seven years ago, I could manage only about a quarter of a mile before I had to stop.

I started to run because I felt desperately unfit.

In those early days I saw few other runners.

In the last two years the London Marathon has become the biggest British sporting event—

What about heart attacks?

My story shows that an unfit 39-year-old, as I was when I started running, who had taken no serious exercise for 20 years, can do the marathon—

I was personally convinced of the health benefits of running

Reassuring evidence now comes from doctors in Seattle, showing that vigorous exercise actually reduces the chances of heart attack.

There is a small risk of unaccustomed stress causing a heart attack when a person is very unfit,

At first, two or three times a week will probably be enough.

When I started running seven years ago, I could manage only about a quarter of a mile before I had to stop. Breathless and aching, I walked the next quarter of a mile, then I jogged the next quarter of a mile, alternating these two activities for a couple of miles. Within a few weeks I could jog half way round Hampstead Heath without stopping. Soon I started to run up the quarter-mile slope to the top of Parliament Hill, although I had to stop at the top to get my breath back. Eventually I found that I could even manage to get up the hill comfortably.

I started to run because I felt desperately unfit. But the biggest pay-off for me was—and still is—the deep relaxation that I achieve by taking exercise. It tires me out but I find that it does calm me down.

In those early days I saw few other runners. Now there are many more—and not just the macho sports freaks. Men and women of all ages have now taken up running. Some 25,000 runners aged five to 85 are attracted each year to the Sunday Times Fun Run in Hyde Park.

In the last two years the London Marathon has become the biggest British sporting event—overtaking the boat race and the Derby in the number of spectators it attracts. When I started to jog I never dreamt of running in a marathon, but in 1982 I realized that if I trained for it, it was within my reach, and after a slow, six-month build-up I managed the 26.2 miles in just under four hours. A creditable performance for a first-timer and a far cry from those days when I had to stop for breath after a quarter of a mile.

What about heart attacks?

My story shows that an unfit 39-year-old, as I was when I started running, who had taken no serious exercise for 20 years, can do the marathon—and that this is a sport in which women can beat men. But is it crazy to do it? Does it make sense to run in the expectation of becoming healthier? What about the chances of injuring yourself or dying of a heart attack?

I was personally convinced of the health benefits of running because I felt unfit, and I wasn't worried about the risk of a heart attack, because I was not a smoker and I was sticking to a fairly low animal-fat diet. But one person I knew well did die immediately after a jog and plenty of people told me I was mad to start running.

Reassuring evidence now comes from doctors in Seattle, showing that vigorous exercise actually reduces the chances of heart attack. They found that people who had a sudden heart attack when they appeared to be completely fit had taken less exercise than those of similar age. According to their findings, published in the *Journal of the American Medical Association* (volume 248, p 3113) it is necessary to take 20 minutes of vigorous exercise at least two or three days a week to obtain some protection from heart attack. Apart from jogging, the exercise might be swimming, singles tennis or squash, digging or chopping wood. Whatever it is, the exercise should leave you out of breath.

There is a small risk of unaccustomed stress causing a heart attack when a person is very unfit, but this can be reduced if exercise is always increased in easy stages. My advice is: if you are under 40, are healthy and feel well, you can begin as I did by jogging gently until you are out of breath, then walking, and alternating the two for about two miles. Build up the jogging in stages until you can do the whole distance comfortably.

At first, two or three times a week will probably be enough. People over 40 who are in any doubt about their health should see their doctor before starting an exercise programme. Over-40s should begin by making a vigorous walk of at least two miles part of the daily routine. When you can do this comfortably you can start the mixed jogging and walking routine and progress from there. You will have to expect soreness of muscles and joints to begin with. If soreness changes to pain, or if you find that you suffer from deep tiredness which you cannot shake off, then stop jogging for a while and just walk.

Answer these questions *before* you read the complete text.

1 Which of these subjects are discussed in the article?
– The author's recovery from cancer due to running
– Advice on illnesses caused by too much exercise
– Advice on how to start running for exercise
– Advice on how to train for the London Marathon
– Evidence that running is the best way of avoiding a heart attack
– How the author trained himself for the London Marathon

2 Are these statements true or false? Put [T] or [F] in the box next to the sentence.
You don't *know* the answers but you can *guess*.

a. ☐ The author came first in the London Marathon.
b. ☐ Running has always been a popular sport in England.
c. ☐ The author knew someone who died after jogging.
d. ☐ Exercise should leave you breathless if it is to improve your health.
e. ☐ People over 40 shouldn't try running if they haven't done it before.

Reading for specific information

Now read the article quickly.
Check your answers to the questions above. How much did you guess correctly?

Comprehension check

1 How did the author feel when he started running?
2 What for him are the pleasures of running?
3 How much exercise do doctors suggest you should take to avoid a heart attack?

What do you think?

1 Do you think the author's suggestions on how to start running are sensible, or potentially dangerous?
2 How fit are you?
What do you do to keep fit?
3 Is it true that we have become more aware of the need to look after our health in the past few years?
What are some of the things we should and shouldn't do to stay healthy?
Think of these topics: diet/ smoking and drinking/exercise/ work.

Vocabulary

Dictionary work

Here is a list of injuries.
Look them up in your dictionary to check the meaning and the pronunciation, and fill in the chart. Use your imagination to think of a cause for the injuries.

Listening

Pre-listening task

Correct first-aid treatment, if it is given properly and promptly, can save lives.
Of course, if the situation is serious, the first thing to do is seek medical attention.
– How good is your knowledge of first aid?
– What would you do in these circumstances?

1 Someone has a minor burn; should you:
a. put cold water on the burned area?
b. put a tight bandage on it?
c. put butter on it?

2 Someone has a bad burn; should you:
a. put cold water on the burned area?
b. put a tight bandage on it?
c. put a loose, clean covering on?

3 You are the first to arrive at the scene of a car accident; should you:
a. lie the victims flat and keep them warm?
b. avoid moving the victims and keep them warm?

Listening for specific information

T.22 Listen to this interview with a doctor and check your answers.

What do you think?

Doctor Clarke advises people to find out as much as they possibly can about first aid.

1 Do you know how to: give artificial respiration?/stop bleeding?
2 What would you do if someone: is choking?/has an electric shock?/ has swallowed some kind of poison?

Discuss your answers. If you're not sure, find out the right answers.

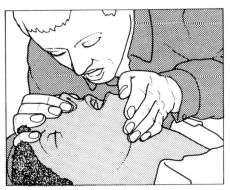

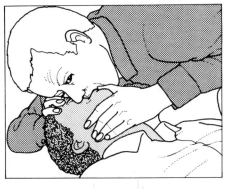

Injury	Cause	Treatment
a broken arm	a fall during a football match	Set the arm and put it in plaster.
a bruise		
a dislocated shoulder		
a sprained wrist		
a sting		
cramp		
a swollen ankle		
concussion		
a blister		
a black eye		
a burn		

● Speaking

Discussion

Here is a list of controversial statements about medical care.
For each one, discuss the advantages and disadvantages.
Think also what the consequences of the idea would be.
These are often neither good nor bad, but are interest points.

1 The State should pay for all medical care. There should be no private medical care.
2 Heart transplants should be stopped. They are rarely successful, and the money could be better spent on other things.
3 The tax on cigarettes should be increased to pay for the health care needed by smokers.
4 Health care should be reduced for people over 65.
5 People who are very ill should have the right to decide if they want to die.
6 Doctors should always give patients all the information about their illness and chances of recovery.

● Writing

Linking words

Put one of the following words or phrases into each gap.
There are eleven gaps. Two of the words or phrases aren't used!

as a result/above all/which/before/ and/especially/although/however/ this is why/such as/on the contrary/ if/to

Doing regular exercise can be dangerous, _____ if you are over 40. _____ it is a very good idea to see your doctor _____ starting if you think you are not very fit. Some people try to exercise too vigorously too soon, and _____ they cause themselves injuries _____ can take a long time to heal.

_____, it is not only older people who should take care. Doctors report many injuries _____ backaches, sprained ankles and pulled muscles, which can all be avoided _____ a little care is taken. If you do injure yourself, rest for a while _____ allow your body to recover naturally. _____, don't push yourself because you think it is doing you good. _____, you could do yourself permanent damage.

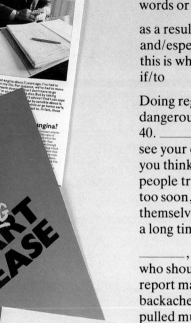

47

UNIT 9

Conditional sentences – First, Second and Zero

Real and unreal conditions

PRESENTATION

Real fears

`T.23A` Gill is going to Germany for a year to be an au pair. Her mother is a little anxious.

Mother Oh dear. I hope everything will be all right. You've never been abroad before.

Gill Don't worry. I'll be OK. I can look after myself.

Mother But what will you do if you don't like the family?

Gill I'll find another one.

Work in pairs. Make up similar dialogues.

These are the other things her mother is worried about:
Perhaps Gill will:
– run out of money.
– be lonely.
– be ill.
– get lost.
– have to work too hard.
Perhaps she won't:
– like the food.
– understand the language.

Imaginary fears

`T.23B`
A What would you do if you saw a ghost?
B I'd run away.
A Wouldn't you talk to it?
B I certainly wouldn't.

Work in pairs. Ask your partner questions.
What would you do if . . .?
– you woke up in the middle of the night and saw a burglar?
– you got stuck in a lift?
– you were given the bill in a restaurant and you realized you didn't have any money?
– you were driving in your car and the brakes failed?
– you had a dream about a plane crash the day before you were going to fly?

48

● Grammar question

What is the difference between the *first* and *second conditional*?

PRACTICE

1 Here is a list of future possibilities. Which do you think are:
a. possible?
b. possible in theory but probably won't happen?

- ☐ rain at the weekend
- ☐ you win a lot of money
- ☐ you are president/leader of your country
- ☐ you have nothing to do tonight
- ☐ your neighbours make a lot of noise this evening
- ☐ you lose your job
- ☐ you have a winter holiday
- ☐ you have three wishes

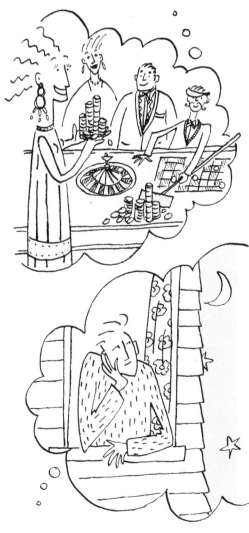

2 Make sentences about these possibilities using either the *first* or *second conditional*.

Example
If it rains this weekend, I'll stay at home./I won't be able to play tennis.
If I won a lot of money, I'd travel round the world./I wouldn't have to go to work.

Pairwork

Student A You are going on holiday. Tell Student B your holiday itinerary and what you hope to do.
Student B You can only see the problems!

Make up a dialogue like this:

A *We're going on a camping holiday this year, to Scotland.*
B *But the weather's awful in Scotland! What will you do if it rains?*
A *We'll …*

A *We hope to do some mountain climbing.*
B *I tried that once. It's very dangerous. What would you do if you fell and hurt yourself?*
A *Well, I'd …*

● Language review

Conditionals: Uses

1 First conditional sentences express **real conditions**.

If I see Peter,	I'll tell him the news.
Possible condition ▶	Result

2 Second conditional sentences express **unreal conditions**.

If I won £10,000,	I'd travel round the world.
Possible, but not probable ▶	Result

The condition is unreal because:
a. It is possible in theory but improbable in practice.
   If I were Prime Minister, I'd increase taxation.
b. It is an impossible speculation.
   If you came from my country you'd understand us better.

Translate

If I see Peter, I'll tell him the news.

If I won some money, I'd travel around the world.

◀ **Look back** at page 48.
Underline the *first conditional* sentences, like this _____.
Underline the *second conditional* sentences, like this _____.

▶ Grammar reference: page 95.

Pre-reading task

Divide into two groups. Make two lists.
1 What will make you live longer?
2 What will make you die sooner?

Think of these areas: job/ambitions/life style/indulgences

Reduce your list to a 'recipe' for long life.
What is your *one* suggestion for longevity?

Intensive reading

Here is a quiz.
First look at the headline and introduction.

– Is the quiz fact or fiction?
– Who wrote the questions?
– Do you think it is serious or light-hearted?

Before you start with the quiz make sure your arithmetic is accurate.

For example:
If you add 2 and 2, what do you get?
If you subtract 5 from 61, what do you get?

Now do the quiz.
You must read every line and do the arithmetic each time.

Example
John lives in London.
Start with the figure   72.
He's male. $\dfrac{3-}{69}$

He lives in a town $\dfrac{2-}{67}$

Now work out how long you can expect to live.

A QUIZ THAT'S AS REALISTIC AS IT'S FASCINATING

So, how long will you live?

WE'RE all going to live longer. Or so the experts tell us. In fact, everybody has the biological capacity to live until they are 100 and collect that telegram from the Queen.
But whether we make the century depends not only on how we treat our bodies but how we live, how we love, how we eat and how we earn. Doctors and insurance companies have devised a set of questions to fix the life expectancy of their patients and clients. What they ask will intrigue and surprise you.
The average lifespan in England and Wales is 69·9 for men, and 76 for women. And just slightly lower in Scotland and Northern Ireland.
So play the life expectancy game. Start with the number 72 and add or subtract according to your answers. Don't worry if the total is not as high as you'd like . . . just adjust that lifestyle and you'll make 100!

START WITH THE FIGURE 72 ...

PERSONAL DATA

If you are male, subtract 3. If female, add 4.
If you live in an urban area with a population over half a million, subtract 2.
If you live in a town of under 10,000, add 2.   76
If any grandparent lived to 85, add 2.   78
If all four grandparents lived, to 80, add 6.
If either parent died of a stroke or heart attack before the age of 50, subtract 4.
If any, parent, brother or sister under 50 has (or had) cancer or a heart condition, or has had diabetes since childhood, subtract 3.
Do you earn more than £25,000 a year? Subtract 2.
If you finished university, add 1. If you have a graduate or professional degree, add 2 more.   81
If you are 63 or over and still working, add 3.
If you live with a spouse or friend, add 5. If not, subtract 1 for every ten years alone since 25.

LIFE STYLE DATA

If you work behind a desk, subtract 3.
If your work requires physical labour, add 3.
If you exercise strenuously (tennis, running, swimming, etc) five times a week for at least half an hour, add 4.
Two or three times a week, add 2.   83
Do you sleep more than 10 hours each night? Subtract 4.
Are you intense, aggressive? Subtract 3.
Are you easy-going and relaxed? Add 3.   86
Are you happy? Add 1. Unhappy? Subtract 2.   87
Have you been booked for speeding in the last year? Subtract 1.
Do you smoke more than two packets of cigarettes a day? Subtract 8. One to two packets? Subtract 6. One half to one packet? Subtract 3.
If you drink one or two whiskies, half a litre of wine, or four glasses of beer a day, add 3.
If you don't drink every day, add 1.   88
If you are a heavy drinker, subtract 8.
Are you overweight by 50 lbs or more? Subtract 8. By 30 to 50 lbs? Subtract 4. By 10 to 30 lbs? Subtract 2.
If you are a man over 40 and have annual check-ups, add 2.
If you are a woman and see a gynaecologist once a year, add 2.
If you prefer simple food, vegetables and fruit to richer, meatier fatty food, and if you always stop eating before you're full, add 1.

AGE ADJUSTMENT

If you are between 30 and 40, add 2.
If you are between 40 and 50, add 3.
If you are between 50 and 70, add 4.
If you are over 70, add 5.

Add up your score for your life expectancy   91

The questionnaire is adapted from the book Lifegain, written by Robert F. Allen and Shirley Linde and published in the USA.

Conversion table
10 lbs = 4.5 kg
30 lbs = 13.5 kg
50 lbs = 22.5 kg

Comprehension check

Compare your life expectancy with other students.
Where did they score or lose points?

What do you think?

1 Read the introduction and the quiz again, and mark it like this.
   This doesn't surprise me = √
   This surprises me   = !!
2 Does the quiz mention any of the topics that you mentioned during the discussion on page 50?
3 What messages does the quiz have about how to live longer?
4 Are they similar to your recipe for long life?

Speaking

Proverbs

1 Discuss and explain the following proverbs.

Example
Many hands make light work.
If people work together, the job will be done quickly.

a. All things in moderation, and moderation in all things.
b. A fool and his money are soon parted.
c. People who live in glass houses shouldn't throw stones.
d. Don't look a gift horse in the mouth.
e. Make hay while the sun shines.
f. Too many cooks spoil the broth.
g. A rolling stone gathers no moss.
h. A stitch in time saves nine.
i. All work and no play makes Jack a dull boy.

2 Translate some of the proverbs you have in your language.
   Do any of them contradict each other?
   Many hands make light work.
   Too many cooks spoil the broth.

Discussion

What would you do in the following situations? Say why.

1 If you were offered two jobs, one which was interesting but badly paid, and one which was boring but well paid, which one would you accept?
2 If you won £5,000, would you give any of it away?
   How much of it would you spend and how much would you save?
3 If you found a wallet in the street with £1,000 in it, and the name (but not the address) of the person who had lost it, what would you do?
4 If you had a son or daughter who wanted to marry someone of a different nationality, colour or religion, what would you do?
5 What would you do if you saw someone shoplifting, for example, stealing food from a supermarket?
6 If you saw a fight in the street what would you do?
7 If you came home and found someone burgling your house, what would you do?
8 If a close friend said 'If anyone asks, tell them I spent the whole of yesterday evening with you', – but they hadn't – what would you do?

Vocabulary

Here is a list of factors you might consider when deciding on a house to buy.
Add your own ideas, and put them in order of importance for yourself.
If you think location is the most important factor, put 1 in the box next to it.

☐ Price
☐ Number of bedrooms
☐ Location
☐ Near to public transport
☐ New
☐ Old
☐ Condition
☐ Garden
☐ Central heating
☐ Size of living room
☐ Separate dining room
☐ Nice views
☐ Sunny

_____

_____

_____

_____

Work in pairs. Compare your list with your partner's.
Ask why did he/she choose that order? Justify your own order.

What particular features would you like your house to have? Be realistic!

open fire-places	shutters
air-conditioning	fitted carpets
patio	fitted wardrobes
balcony	loft space
double-glazing	utility room

51

Listening

T.24 You will hear a dialogue between a married couple, Linda and Jeremy, who are talking about a house that they have just seen and that they are thinking of buying. They don't always agree.

Comprehension check

1 Listen to the tape and fill in the chart.

Linda's opinion

Location _____

_____

_____

Lounge _____

_____

_____

Kitchen _____

_____

_____

Bedrooms _____

_____

_____

Jeremy's opinion

Location _____

_____

_____

_____

Lounge _____

_____

_____

_____

Kitchen _____

_____

_____

Bedrooms _____

_____

_____

2 What is Linda's general impression of the house? What is Jeremy's?
3 Describe the house that they are talking about. Give the *facts*, not their opinions.

Language work

Complete these sentences from the tape.

If we _____ this house, we _____ have to drive to the station.
If the ceilings _____ lower in our house now, it _____ be much cheaper to heat.
If they _____ do something about the roof soon, the ceiling _____ come down.

Writing

Description

Describe this house briefly. How old do you think it is? How much do you think it is worth? £20,000?/£200,000?/£2,000,000?

Now read this description.

The house is situated at the bottom of the Chess valley next to the River Chess. It's about 20 miles from London and just outside the village of Chorleywood. It's a really splendid period property. The oldest parts are Elizabethan, but there were some additions in the 1820s.

It seems typically English to me. There are long corridors and huge oak-panelled rooms, and you can imagine all sorts of scenes from history taking place here.

52

As you come in through the front door, you find yourself in a large hall with an open fireplace, which is unusual. One of the doors on the right of the hall leads into the living room. This room faces south, so it's very sunny, and it has a lovely view of the whole valley. The furniture has been chosen to match the style of the house, so there's a lot of leather and dark, heavy wood. Next to this room there's the dining room which has French windows leading onto a small patio.

Also on the ground floor there is a study, kitchen and utility room. A wide staircase takes you to the first floor, where there are five bedrooms. The largest is about 25′ × 20′, a really vast room which looks out onto the garden.

The house is in 2.5 acres of land, and there is a green house, a shed, a swimming-pool and a tennis court.

It's a beautiful place to be at any time of year. In winter it's warm and cosy and in summer there's so much to do outside.

1 The description is in five paragraphs.
 What is the purpose of each one?

2 Go through the text again and underline like this
 _____ what is *factual description* and like this _ _ _ _ _ what is *personal opinion*.
 Sometimes the same sentence may be part fact and part opinion.

3 Box like this ☐☐☐☐ all the prepositions (and prepositional phrases) of place:
 ☐ at the bottom ☐

4 How many different rooms are mentioned?
a. What do you do in each room?
b. Are there any rooms not mentioned?

5 Circle like this ⬭ any words or expressions that you think are special to the description of a house:
 ⬭corridors⬭ ⬭leads into⬭

6 There are several Imperial measurements in the text. Here are their equivalents in Metric.

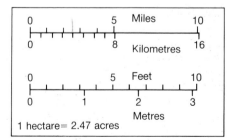

7 Now write a description of a house or a flat. Include the following
– facts and physical description
– your impressions and opinions
– a description of some of the rooms.

UNIT 10

Expressing Ability and Permission

Ability, past present and future

PRESENTATION

Here is the nine o'clock news.

T.25 Last night thieves stole a painting from the home of Lord Bonniford. The painting, a sixteenth-century masterpiece by Holbein, is said to be priceless. Lord Bonniford said he could hear noises in the middle of the night, but he paid no attention. The security guard, Mr Charles Potts, couldn't phone the police because he was tied hand and foot.

The thieves managed to get in and escape without setting off the security alarm by cutting off the electricity supply.

Andrew Gardener, the man who had a liver, heart and kidney transplant, is doing well after his operations, say his doctors.
Andrew is able to sit up and feed himself. He can get out of bed but he can't walk yet, as he is still too weak. Doctors say he'll be able to go home in a few weeks' time.

● Grammar question

Underline all the verbs that express ability.
What is the difference between them?

54

PRACTICE

Use the verbs you underlined. Fill each gap with one of these verbs, in the correct tense.

Sinclair has introduced a new home computer, the Electron 2000. It _____ answer the telephone, but it _____ understand human speech. Clive Sinclair hopes to bring out a computer next year which _____ do this.

Two prisoners escaped from Wandsworth prison yesterday. Warders _____ stop them because they were locked in a bathroom. The prisoners _____ climb the 30-foot wall by using a home-made ladder.

Pairwork

Write similar news stories for these headlines.
Include some ability structures.

JET CRASH-300 ESCAPE

Pilot misses one plane, but hits another.

MIRACLE RECOVERY

7-year-old Alison, deaf since birth, hears for the first time.

MILKMAN RESCUES BOY FROM BLAZE

INVENTION ALLOWS SCIENTIST TO CONTROL WEATHER

Permission

PRESENTATION

T.26

A Could I go home early, Steve? I don't feel very well.
B Yes, of course. What's the matter?
A I feel dizzy.

A Do you mind if I open the window? It's a bit stuffy in here.
B No, not at all. Please do.
A Thank you.

A Would you mind if I borrowed your paper?
B Actually, I'm just going to read it myself. Sorry.
A Never mind. It doesn't matter.

Grammar questions

Underline with a solid line _____ the different verbs that ask for permission.
Underline with a broken line _ _ _ _ _ the different ways of giving permission.
How does **B** (in conversation 3) refuse permission?

PRACTICE

Pairwork

Make up similar dialogues.
Student A You have a room in Student B's house.
Student B You are a landlord/ landlady.

If you are *asking for permission* or *refusing permission*, give a reason if appropriate.

Student A wants to
– borrow B's newspaper
– turn the television on
– turn the volume up
– change the channel
– have a party on Saturday
– stick some pictures on the wall
– have a pet in the room
– move the furniture round

Listen

T.27 *Could I go?*
Would you mind if I went? (More formal)
I want to do something.
I'm asking your permission.

Could you help me?
Would you mind helping me? (More formal)
I want *you* to do something.
I'm asking you to do it for me.

T.28 Listen to these dialogues. A man called Dick is talking to five different people.
On a separate piece of paper write down the answers to these questions.
a. Where are they?
b. Who is Dick talking to?
c. Is Dick asking for permission, or is he asking someone to do something for him?

Expressing ability

Can and be able to express ability.
I can type but I can't do short-hand.
I'll be able to walk again when the
plaster is taken off my leg.

Could is the past tense of can.
I could swim when I was four.

Translate

I can swim.

I could swim when I was four.

I'll be able to walk again soon.

● Language review 2

Asking for permission.
Can/Could I go home early, please?

More formal and distant:
Do/Would you mind if I open/
opened the window, please?

Translate

Could I go home, please?

Would you mind if I opened the
window, please?

▶ Grammar reference: page 96.

SKILLS DEVELOPMENT
● Reading

Pre-reading task

Look at the headline, and try to put
one word (of *your* choice) into each
gap.

Ruth Lawrence, aged 10, has come
_____ in a mathematics
examination out of 530 other
students, all hoping to go to St
Hugh's College, Oxford. She has
already _____ her maths A-level,
but admitted that she was a bit

_____ to do so well in the entrance
exam. She will go to Oxford at the
_____ of 12. The Principal of the
college said 'She is obviously
_____.'

How Ruth made history at Oxford

by Isabel Hilton

1 CHILD PRODIGY Ruth Lawrence
made history yesterday when she came a
clear first out of the 530 candidates who
sat the entrance exam for St. Hugh's
College, Oxford. The all-women's college
is likely to offer her a scholarship. Ruth
sat three three-hour papers—Algebra and
Geometry; Calculus, Probability and
Statistics; and Maths, Pure and Applied.
'I was happy with the first two,' she said
yesterday, 'but I wasn't sure about the
third.'

2 Ruth, who lives in Huddersfield, has
never been to school. Her father, Harry
Lawrence, a computer consultant, gave

up his job when Ruth was five to educate
her at home. Her mother, Sylvia, who
also works in computers, is the family
breadwinner.

3 Harry Lawrence explained that,
besides mathematics, Ruth also enjoyed
English, history, geography, nature study
and other subjects. She began to read at
four and started academic subjects at five.
'We did not start off with the thought
that she would not go to school,' he said,
'but we enjoyed teaching her so much and
we seemed to be making quite a good job
of it, so we just carried on.'

4 Because she does not go to school, Ruth
has not mixed much with other children.
'She enjoys serious conversation with
adults,' her father said, 'and I don't think
she will feel out of place at Oxford.' He
does not think she works harder than
other children her age, but concentrates
on what she enjoys, principally mathematics. 'She watches television a little but
not as a habit', he explained. 'But she
plays the piano and has quite a wide range
of interests.'

5 If she does well at St Hugh's, Ruth
expects to take a further degree and
eventually hopes to become a research
professor in mathematics—an ambition
she may achieve while still in her teens.
The Lawrence family plans to move to
Oxford when Ruth takes up her place in
October 1983. Before then, she plans to
take four A levels to satisfy the college
matriculation requirements. Her father
hopes she will be exempt from the
requirement to pass a foreign language—a
'diversion', he feels, 'from her main
interest'.

6 Miss Rachel Trickett, the principal of
St Hugh's, said last night: 'We are all
very excited about Ruth. She is obviously
quite brilliant and has shown genuine
originality.' Ruth's future tutor, Dr
Glenys Luke, admits that taking so young
a student is a daunting responsibility but
says it is one she expects to enjoy. 'I shall
tailor the teaching to her requirements',
she said. 'Ruth shouldn't have to suffer
the same tensions and disappointments
that older students face. I hope I shall
make it fun for her.'

7 Last night the Lawrence family were
thrilled at Ruth's achievement. 'We all
jumped up and down a bit when we
heard', said Harry Lawrence. When Ruth
becomes a student, Harry Lawrence looks
forward to concentrating his efforts on
her younger sister Rebecca, seven. 'She's
doing very well,' he said, 'but it's too
early to tell whether she's a mathematician.'

Reading for specific information

Read the article and make a list of
the things that make Ruth unusual
for a ten year old.

4 Mathematics.
5 Yes, she does. She plays the piano.
6 She said, 'She is obviously quite brilliant.'
7 Dr Glenys Luke.
8 He's going to help Ruth's sister in a similar way.

Vocabulary

Adverbs of intensity

Example
Ruth is clever.
*She's **very** clever.*
Ruth is brilliant.
*She's **absolutely** brilliant.*

Very and ***absolutely*** are adverbs of **intensity**.

Note: We do not use **very** with adjectives like 'brilliant' because 'brilliant' already means 'very clever'. Other examples of such strong adjectives are: *freezing, exhausted, fascinating, disgusting*. If we want to intensify an extreme adjective we need an adverb like '*absolutely*'.

Example
I've found his explanation *absolutely fascinating*.

1 Match each adjective in the left-hand column with its stronger equivalent from the right-hand column.

1	hot	a	vast
2	cold	b	terrified
3	interesting	c	disgusting
4	dirty	d	filthy
5	tasty	e	exhausted
6	bad	f	boiling
7	frightened	g	hilarious
8	big	h	fascinating
9	angry	i	freezing
10	tired	j	furious
11	surprised	k	astonished
12	funny	l	delicious

2 In pairs make up dialogues like this to practise the vocabulary.
  A *I was very surprised when I heard the news about . . .*
  B *I was absolutely astonished!*
Here are some possible topics:
a meal/a film/a book/a person/a journey/the weather

Comprehension check

1 What role do Ruth's mother and father play in her upbringing?
2 Why did they decide to educate her at home?
3 What is Ruth's ambition?
4 How old will she be when she achieves this ambition?
5 How will the college change the course for Ruth?
6 What was the Lawrence family's reaction to the news?

What do you think?

1 Work in pairs and compare the lists you made while you were reading.
2 Do you agree about what makes Ruth unusual?
3 'Ruth has not mixed much with other children.'
Do you think this is important?
4 What were your interests when you were ten?

Summarizing

Match the summary to the correct paragraph.

☐ a. Her father has been her teacher, while her mother goes out to work.
☐ b. The university tutors are very pleased that Ruth is coming and are going to change the course a little to suit her.
☐ c. She wants to be a research professor. Before university she hopes to take four more A-levels.
☐ d. Ruth's academic background.
☐ e. She made history by coming first, but she herself wasn't happy with all the examination papers.
☐ f. Her family are very excited and wonder if the younger sister will be as talented.
☐ g. The kind of person that Ruth is. Her likes and interests.

Language work

Here are the answers to some questions about Ruth.
In pairs, work out the questions.

1 A computer consultant.
2 Her mother.
3 She was four.

Listening

T.29 Listen to this interview about educating children at home. The interviewer talks to Bruce Cox, who is a member of an organization called *Education Otherwise*.

While you are listening, take notes under these headings.
- The reasons why Mr Cox didn't send his children to an ordinary school.
- How his children's education is organized.
- The kind of alternative school they do go to.

Compare your notes with another student. Listen to the tape again to check.

Speaking

Roleplay

Work in groups.
There was another member of the discussion, June Fisher, who is Head Teacher at a comprehensive school, but you didn't hear her. She strongly disagreed with Bruce Cox.

List the reasons against educating your children at home.
Think of what she might have said in reply. Consider these aspects:
- Qualifications of parents
- The children's development
- The role of schools
- Exams and qualifications

Pair up with a student from another group.
One of you is Bruce Cox, the other June Fisher.
Continue the discussion.

Discussion

1 Do you think Bruce Cox's children are getting a good education?
2 Did you enjoy your education? Bruce Cox said, 'I think many people didn't do very many activities (at school) for the enjoyment and pleasure of doing them.'
Is this true for you?
Is it the role of schools to provide 'enjoyment and pleasure'?

3 What do you understand by the 'carrot and stick' motivation?
4 The interviewer said, 'I would have loved to have been educated like that.'
What about you?
Would you have liked *your* parents to be your teachers?
5 Would you like to educate your children at home?

Writing

Here is a jumbled letter of complaint, without an opening or closing paragraph.
Put it in the correct order, and paragraph is appropriately.

Which of these opening and closing paragraphs do you think is the most appropriate?
Say why.

Opening
1 The time has come when I have really had enough of all this bad workmanship and the bad service you have to take as a consumer in this country.
2 I feel I must complain to you about the service I have received from both your shop assistants and your office staff.
3 I am very angry and fed up, and being a student I do not have much money anyway.

Closing
1 So get in touch soon or they will cause you a lot of trouble.
2 Please help me soon, because all my friends said how much that style of shoe suited me.
3 I hope to hear from you before I have to write to them.

1 Since then I have written to you twice, and have tried to phone on several occasions, but I have had no reply.

2 Naturally I took them back to the shop.

3 They cost £34.99, which I do not think is cheap.

4 This organisation often prosecutes shops that sell faulty goods.

5 However, after only three weeks I had to have them re-heeled.

6 If I do not hear from you in the next two weeks, I will get in touch with the Consumer Advice Bureau.

7 I bought a pair of shoes from your Oxford Street branch on 17 September last.

8 I said that I did not want to choose another style, and that I wanted my money back.

9 For a pair of shoes at this price, one would expect them to last several years.

10 There I was told that I could have another pair of shoes, but that particular style was out of stock.

11 Not only that, but they began to leak in rainy weather.

12 The shop assistant informed me that she could not do this, and that if I wanted a refund I had to write to your office.

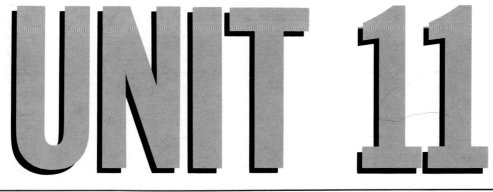

UNIT 11

Present Perfect Continuous

NICKY'S
ABINGDON 30824

Life-long passions

PRESENTATION

T.30 Betty Tudor's life-long
passion is driving, but there's a
problem, as our interviewer found
out.

Interviewer How long have you
  been trying to pass your driving
  test, Betty?
Betty Seventeen years.
Interviewer And how many times
  have you taken it?

Betty Thirty-eight, and I'm afraid
  I've failed it every time. I've always
  wanted to be able to drive, and I'm
  determined to pass.
Interviewer I suppose you've been
  having lessons all this time.
Betty That's right.
Interviewer How many have you
  had?
Betty Over two hundred and
  seventy. It's cost me about two
  thousand pounds already. I'm
  taking the test again next week.
Interviewer I hear you're saving up
  to buy your own car. How long
  have you been saving?

Betty Since 1982.
Interviewer And how much have
  you saved?
Betty Over £4,000, and that's
  enough to buy a nice little second-
  hand car.
Interviewer Well, all the very best
  with your next test.
Betty Thank you.

● Grammar questions

Underline with a solid line _____
the examples of the *Present Perfect
Simple*.
Underline with a broken line
_ _ _ _ the examples of the *Present
Perfect Continuous*.

Why does the interviewer ask:
How long have you been saving?
but
How much have you saved?

PRACTICE

1 Betty Tudor doesn't use full
   sentences when answering the
   interviewer's questions which
   begin *How . . .?*
   Complete her sentences like this:
   *I have been trying to pass my
   driving test for seventeen years.*
2 Write similar interviews with these
   two people about their life-long
   passions, using the information
   below.
   Ask questions beginning with:
   How long . . .?
   How many . . .?

59

Gina Mellish.
Opera singer.
Married three times.
Works with New York Opera Company.

Henry Blofeld.
Stamp collector.
Collected over 20,000 stamps.
Works for philatelist publisher.
Has the world famous Penny Blue.

Pairwork

Interview each other. Ask questions beginning *How long...?*
You must decide whether to use the *Present Perfect Simple* or *Continuous*.

a. know/teacher?
b. work/as a...?
c. live in...?
d. study/this book?
e. have your car/watch/ring?
f. play/squash/tennis/rubgy?
g....

Results of past activity

PRESENTATION

T.31

A You look tired. What have you been doing?
B I'm exhausted. I've been getting ready to go on holiday.

A Have you done everything?
B Nearly. I've packed the cases, and I've been to the bank, but I haven't checked the flight yet.

● Grammar questions

Underline with a solid line ———
the examples of the *Present Perfect Simple*.
Underline with a broken line
_ _ _ _ _ the examples of the *Present Perfect Continuous*.

Why does **A** ask:
What have you been doing?
but
Have you done everything?

PRACTICE

Pairwork

1 Make up similar dialogues, using the prompts below.

Example
covered in paint
decorating the living room

A You're covered in paint! What have you been doing?
B I've been decorating the living room.
A Have you finished it?
B Not yet. I've painted the woodwork, but I haven't put up the wallpaper yet.

a. oil on your face
   servicing the car
b. dirty hands
   working in the garden
c. blood on your finger
   sawing wood – making a book case
d. eyes are bloodshot
   revising for an exam
e. smell of garlic
   cooking

2 There is something wrong with these sentences. Discuss with another student why they're wrong, and say what would be better.
a. I've been cutting my finger.
b. I've read *War and Peace* this afternoon.
c. It's easy to stop smoking. I've been giving up many times.

d. I'm terribly sorry, Mr Brown, but I've been crashing into the back of your car.
e. Could you help me? I've been losing my passport.

Language review

The Present Perfect Continuous: Uses

The *Present Perfect Continuous*, like the *Simple*, relates past activities to the present. It has two uses:

1 To express **unfinished past**.
I've been working here for fifteen years.
How long have you been learning English?

See the diagram on page 38. There is little difference between the *Simple* and *Continuous*, but remember the verbs that rarely take the *Continuous*. (See page 88.)

2 To express the **present result** of past activities.
A *You look tired. What have you been doing?*
B *I've been doing the housework.*
Here the *Continuous* stresses the **activity**.
B *I've cleaned the bathroom and I've done the washing up.*
Here the *Simple* stresses the **completed action**.

Translate

I work in London.

_____

I've been working here for fifteen years.

_____

Before that I worked in America.

_____

You look tired. What have you been doing?

_____

I've been cleaning the house.

_____

I cleaned it last week, too.

_____

▶ Grammar reference: page 97.

H/W — read p 97, sentences p 57 and letter p. 58.

SKILLS DEVELOPMENT

Speaking

Roleplay

In pairs, prepare a conversation by following through the flow chart.

Student A meets **Student B**

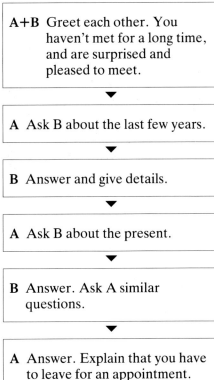

A+B Greet each other. You haven't met for a long time, and are surprised and pleased to meet.
▼
A Ask B about the last few years.
▼
B Answer and give details.
▼
A Ask B about the present.
▼
B Answer. Ask A similar questions.
▼
A Answer. Explain that you have to leave for an appointment.
▼
B Say you regret this.
▼
A+B Arrange to meet again soon.
▼
A+B Say goodbye.

Listening

Pre-listening task

Have you ever given money to charity or worked for a charity? Look at this list of charities and charitable causes.
Which do you think are the most and least deserving?

– Help the Aged
– National Society for the Prevention of Cruelty to Children
– Royal Society for the Prevention of Cruelty to Animals
– Cancer research
– A group that protests against experiments on animals
– A local child who needs an expensive operation in America

Listening for gist

T.32   Listen to these four different charity appeals.

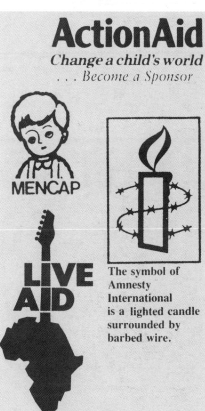

ActionAid
Change a child's world
... *Become a Sponsor*

MENCAP

LIVE AID

The symbol of Amnesty International is a lighted candle surrounded by barbed wire.

Comprehension check

For each of the charities, say
– which people it tries to help
– why these people need help
– how the charity tries to help them
– the charity's successes and problems

What do you think?

If you had £1,000 that you wanted to give to charity, which of these four would you give to? How would you divide the money?

First decide on your own which charity or charities you would give to. Then discuss with a partner until the two of you agree. Finally try to come to a decision as a class.

61

Reading

Look at these pictures, and discuss the ways in which charities raise money from the public.

Scan reading

Read this newspaper article and answer these questions as quickly as possible.

a. Is Nicky raising money for an international or a local cause?
b. How is she going to do it?
c. What will the money be spent on?
d. There is a play on words in the headline. Find it and explain it.

Now read the article in more depth.

Nurse Nicky nears her peak of fitness

There are different ways of training to climb Kilimanjaro, Africa's highest mountain.

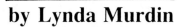

by Lynda Murdin

Nurse Nicky Bennett-Rees has been walking across London every day from her flat to Great Ormond Street Hospital. Then, once her night-shift nursing sick children is over, she runs the five and half miles back home. Every weekend for the past two months she has been jogging in the park and playing her favourite sport, tennis. 'I've even changed my diet', she explained. 'Now it's steak, eggs and as much fresh fruit as I can eat.'

Climb for money

What's it all for? Nicky is taking part in a sponsored climb at the beginning of September to raise money for an extension to the children's ward at her hospital. She and nine others (including myself) will spend five days climbing up and down Kilimanjaro's 19,340 feet. This is a final attempt to raise the £250,000 they need to build accommodation for the families of children desperately ill in hospital. They have been trying to raise the money for five years, and have so far collected nearly £200,000.

Separated

Nurse Nicky knows just how valuable it can be for children to have their parents near at such times. She has seen how parents of sick children are separated from the rest of their families, and then have to sleep on waiting-room floors.

'It's great to be able to do something like this and at the same time make money for a worthwhile cause,' she added.

All the members of the climb have something in common. They have all had major surgery at some time in their lives, but there are no doubts about their fitness. They have all been training under Terry Allen, a football coach.

Donations

Such a trip needs a lot of organization and funding, and help has come from many quarters. Special winter clothing will be needed on the snow-covered summit, and local shops have provided this, and also climbing boots, sleeping bags, and water bottles. The Dutch airline KLM has donated five of the air tickets to Tanzania free of charge.

Since this newspaper announced the climb two weeks ago, readers have sent in scores of coupons like the one below. But more support is needed. Now is your chance to sponsor a worthy cause, so fill the coupon in now.

I wish to sponsor the Sick Children's Trust Kilimanjaro Project team £.... p.... per 1000 ft.

Total ....

Signature

Name ....

Address ....

Phone No. ....

SEND to Dr John Pritchard, The Sick Children's Trust, Home from Home, 139 Gray's Inn Road, London WC1X 8UB.

Next week I'll tell you how I've been preparing for the climb!

Comprehension check/Language work

1 How has Nicky been training for the climb?
2 How many people are going to take part in the climb?
3 What do they all have in common?
4 How long have they been trying to raise the money?
5 Complete this sentence.
So far they _____ nearly £200,000
6 What donations has the group already received?
7 Read the text again.
Underline like this _____ the examples of the *Present Perfect Simple*.
Underline like this _ _ _ _ _ the examples of the *Present Perfect Continuous*.
Explain *why* each tense is used.
8 Imagine you are the writer of this article. How have *you* been preparing for the climb?

What do you think?

1 Do you think this is a worthy cause?
Why?
2 If you decided to sponsor them, how much would you sponsor them for?
If they completed the climb, how much would it cost you?
3 What do you understand by these?
'Charity begins at home.' (English proverb)
'We give to other people not for the good we wish to do them but for the good we wish to do for ourselves.' (Seventeenth-century French writer)
Do you agree?

Vocabulary

Compound nouns

a staff room   a waiting-room
a changing room   a reading-room

– Who are these rooms for?
– Where do you find them?
– Can you think of any more kinds of room?

Words can be combined to make new words.

They are written in different ways.
bedroom (one word)
cough mixture (two words)
face-lift (hyphenated)

There are no rules, and English people themselves often have to consult the dictionary for the correct spelling.
The stress is normally on the first word.
Find the compound nouns on page 62.

1 Can you guess the words? Check in the dictionary to see if you're right.

a. What do you use to clean or wash the following?
your teeth/shoes/clothes/dishes
b. What do you have in your hands for these sports?
tennis/golf/fishing/squash/hockey/baseball
c. Make as many compounds as you can with these words the *second* word.
cup/glasses/book/bottle/card/paper/machine

2 How many of the objects in this picture can you name?
A lot of them are compound nouns.

63

Writing

The style of formal letters

Here are two letters to a bank manager.

Compare them and say which one you prefer.

One contains mistakes of style. It is too informal, it is badly organised and it has irrelevant information. With a partner, compare them carefully for stylistic variations.

Write a letter to a bank, requesting a loan to buy a new car.

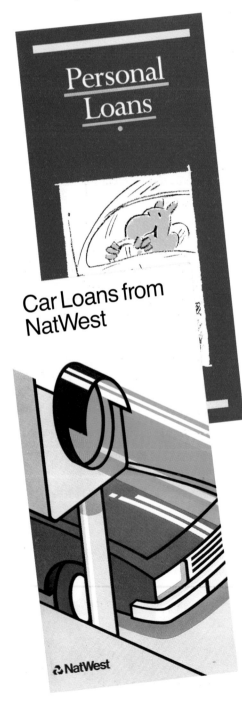

Personal Loans

Car Loans from NatWest

NatWest

Dear Mr Henderson,

I have been working as a librarian for two years at the Central Records Office, but I do not feel that I wish to make this my career.

A friend recently told me about a course that the Oxford Business School offers, and it sounds most interesting. I am told that employers respect this college and its diploma.

In order to follow this course I would need a loan of approximately £200. Could I make an appointment with you to discuss the possibility of this?

I look forward to hearing from you.

Yours sincerely,

Jeremy Foster

Dear Mr. Henderson,

As you probably know, I have done about two years as a librarian at the Central Records Office, just round the corner from your bank, in fact, but I do not really think it is the sort of job I can do much longer.

Anyway, I was at this party the other day and I met a friend and he told me about a great course you can do at the Oxford Business School, and my brother thinks I would get a good job if I did it.

Do you think I could come and see you, and talk about a bank loan? About £200 would be enough.

I'm looking forward to your letter. I hope you'll say yes.

Yours sincerely,

Jeremy Foster

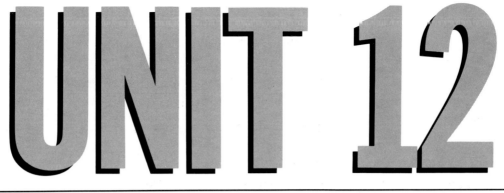

UNIT 12

Future Arrangements and Future Certainty

Arranging to meet

PRESENTATION

Miss Appleby is in the textile business. Here is her diary for today, with her secretary's notes down the side.

T.33 Listen to this telephone call between a businessman and Miss Appleby's secretary. It is 9.30 in the morning. Sometimes the tape stops. Listen carefully and write in the 'Your ideas' column what you think the secretary says.

Friday 15
(227-138) WEEK 33

9.00 – 10.00 Visit factory

10.30 ?11.00? Back in office   Traffic sometimes bad

12.15   Lunch with designer   Very important

2.00 – 2.30 See customer in office

Rest of p.m. In office   Certain

Your ideas

a. She _____ a factory.
b. Well, she _____ late because of the traffic.
c. No, she _____ with a designer.
d. She _____ here in her office.
e. Definitely. She _____ be in her office for the rest of the afternoon.

Now listen to the tape again. This time you will hear all the secretary's words. Copy into the Dictation column the sentences that were missing from the first tape. Compare what you wrote under 'Your ideas' with the dictation.

Dictation from the tape

a. She _____ a factory.
b. Well, she _____ late because of the traffic.
c. No, she _____ with a designer.
d. She _____ here in her office.
e. Definitely. She _____ be in her office for the rest of the afternoon.

● Grammar questions

Look at the sentences from the dictation.
1 Does sentence **a** refer to the present or the future?
  Do sentences **c** and **d** refer to the present or the future?
2 What's the difference in certainty between sentences **b** and **e**?

PRACTICE

Pairwork

Imagine it is Friday, and you need to meet your partner some time over the weekend to discuss some work. First, fill in your own diary. What plans have you made for the weekend?
Decide also when you are free.

	Saturday	Sunday
Morning		
Afternoon		
Evening		

When you are ready, discuss your plans together and see if it is possible to meet. If it is, arrange a time and a place.

Pairwork

A *Where are you going for your holidays this year?*
B *We haven't decided yet. We might go to Greece, or we might go to Italy.*

Student A Ask B the questions.
Student B You haven't made up your mind!

a. travel?
   fly/go by car
b. stay?
   hotel/rent a house
c. How long . . .?
   for a week/for a fortnight
d. When . . .?
   July/August
e. Who . . . with?
   friends/alone

● Language review 1

The Present Continuous for the future

The *Present Continuous* can be used to express a **future arrangement**.
I'm having lunch with Bob today.
She's getting married in the spring.

In the first sentence, the arrangement is in my diary.
In the second sentence, a date has been fixed and the church perhaps booked.

Translate

What are you doing tonight?

I'm having a meal with Alice.

◀ **Look back** at page 65 and underline the examples of the *Present Continuous* with future meaning.

● Language review 2

Degrees of future certainty

Might, could and will express **degrees of certainty** about the future.
He might/could come tomorrow, but I doubt it.
I'm sure he'll come tomorrow.

In the opinion of the speaker, **might** and **could** express a **future possibility**.

Will expresses a **future certainty**.

Might and could also express a **present possibility**.
A *Where's Mary?*
B *I'm not sure. She might/could be upstairs.*

Translate

He might come tomorrow, but I doubt it.

I'm sure he'll come tomorrow.

A Where's Mary?

B She might be upstairs.

◀ **Look back** at page 65 and underline the examples of **might** and **will**.

▶ **Grammar reference:** page 98.

SKILLS DEVELOPMENT

● Reading

Pre-reading task

1 What is happening at the moment in the American, Russian, and European space programmes? What are they planning to do?

2 Look at the pictures of a possible settlement in space. In pairs write some questions. What would you like to know about living in space?

   When will it happen?
   Where will the food come from?

Scan reading

Read the first sentence of each paragraph quickly.
Which paragraph do you think will answer your questions?
Which questions won't be answered?

Reading for specific information

Read the text and find the answers to your questions.
Then re-read and answer the following questions.

Comprehension check

1 The article refers to the flights to the Moon in the 1970s as 'camping trips'. What does this mean?
2 Sheffield is about 150 miles from London. How high above the Earth does the Shuttle orbit?
3 Who produced these plans for a space settlement?
4 Why would gravity be so important?
5 Why is the Moon unsuitable for a settlement?
6 How and why would sunlight be controlled?
7 Why would the settlement look similar to 'modern' small towns on Earth?
8 What is L5?
9 'There could be settlements in space that would house adventurers leading more or less normal lives.' What elements of living in space would be normal? What would be unusual?

LIFE IN

SPACE

We haven't conquered space. Not yet. We have sent some 20 men on camping trips to the Moon, and the USA and the Soviet Union have sent people to spend restricted lives orbiting the Earth. During the next few weeks, for instance, the US Space Shuttle will take Spacelab into orbit, showing that ordinary (non-astronaut) scientists can live and work in space – for a few days only.

All these are marvellous technical and human achievements, but none of them involves living independently in space. The Russians need food and even oxygen sent up from Earth. And they haven't gone far into space. The residents of Sheffield are farther from London than those of the Shuttle or the Soviet's Salyut. It is only in fiction, and in space movies, that people spend long periods living more or less normally deep in space.

But in a couple of decades – by the year 2000, say – this could have changed. There could be settlements in space that would house adventurers leading more or less normal lives.

The picture on this page shows where the settlers would live. It seems like science fiction – but it is not. It is based on plans produced by hard-headed people: engineers and scientists, headed by Gerard O'Neill of Princeton University, summoned to a conference by NASA. They are space enthusiasts, of course, but they are not dreamers.

The settlement is a gigantic wheel, a tube more than 400ft in diameter bent into a ring just over a mile across. The wheel spins gently once a minute. It is this gentle rotation that makes this settlement different from the Shuttle and Salyut, and infinitely different from the Lunar modules that took man for the first time to any non-terrestrial soil, because the spin produces a force that feels like gravity. Every space trip has shown that the human body needs gravity if it isn't to deteriorate, and gravity also makes normal activities possible. Nobody would want to live for long in a space settlement where everything – people and equipment and the eggs they were trying to fry – moved weightlessly around.

With gravity, life in space can be based on our experience on Earth. We can have farming and factories and houses and meeting-places that are not designed by guesswork. ▷

The need for gravity is one of the reasons for building a space colony, rather than sending settlers to an existing location such as the Moon or the planets. The Moon is inhospitable. Its gravity is tiny – and any one place on the Moon has 14 days of sunlight followed by 14 of night, which makes agriculture impossible and means there is no using solar energy.

In the settlement, which floats in permanent sunlight, the day-length is controlled. A gigantic mirror about a mile in diameter floats weightlessly above the ring of the settlement. It reflects sunlight on to smaller mirrors that direct it into the ring, through shutters that fix the day length.

The sunlight is constant during the 'daytime', so farming is productive to an extent which can be reached on Earth only occasionally. The aim is to provide a diet similar to that on Earth, but with less fresh meat.

The farms will be arranged in terraces with fish ponds and rice paddies in transparent tanks on the top layer; wheat below; vegetables, soya, and maize below that.

The population of the settlement is fixed at about 10,000 people: farm output can be accurately planned. Research reports suggest that about 44 square metres of vegetables will be needed for each person, and just over five square metres of pastures.

The picture here shows where the people will live. It doesn't look very different from modern small towns on Earth, and this is deliberate. Science-fiction films feature vast glass tower blocks and subterranean warrens, but real-life space settlers won't want these. Throughout history, settlers have tried to put up buildings like the ones they left behind, because these are familiar: space settlers will do the same.

And where would the settlement be? 'Why', say the experts, 'at L5, of course.' This reference describes a point on the Moon's orbit around the Earth, equidistant from Moon and Earth, where the gravitational forces of the two bodies balance. (The L stands for Lagrange, a French mathematician who listed a number of 'balance' points.) Those who intend to settle in space have formed an L5 Society. The members are not all impractical eccentrics: that is, they are not all impractical.

68

What do you think?

1 The article does not say what would occupy people's time in space. What do you think they could do?
2 No reasons are given why there should be settlements in space. What reasons can you think of?
3 Does the article make living in space sound attractive? What would appeal to you?
4 Do you think the expense of such space programmes is justified?

Vocabulary

Phrasal verbs

Phrasal verbs consist of a **verb** and a **preposition** or **adverb**.

to put on/to look up/to make up/look after

Do you know a phrasal verb to replace the words in italics?
The rocket *left the ground* smoothly.
The astronaut *moved the switch on* his radio.
He is *trying to find* minerals on the Moon.

There are three main types of phrasal verbs. It is important to know which type a phrasal verb is in order to know how to use it.
A dictionary tells you this.

Type 1

take off, (a) make a start in jumping. (b) (of an air-craft) leave the ground and rise: *The plane took off despite the fog.*

There is no object.

Type 2

turn sth on, start the flow of (liquid, gas, current) by ~ing a tap, switch, etc: *T~ the lights/radio on.*

The position of 'sth' (=something) before 'on' tells you the object can change position.

Type 3

look for sb/sth, (a) search for; try to find: *Are you still ~ing for a job?*

The position of 'sb' (=somebody) and 'sth' after 'for' tells you the object cannot change position.

1 Which type of phrasal verb are the following?

blow up, (a) explode: *The barrel of gunpowder blew up.* (b) arise: *A storm is ~ing up.* (c) lose one's temper; work up to a crisis: *I'm sorry I blew up at you.* ~ **sb up,** (colloq) scold severely: *The teacher blew John up for not doing his homework.* Hence, **~-ing-'up** n scolding. ~ **sth up,** (a) break or destroy by explosion: *The soldiers blew up the bridge.* (b) inflate with air or gas: *~ up a tyre.* (c) enlarge greatly: *~ up a photograph.*

carry (sth) on, continue (doing sth) : *C~ on (with your work). They decided to ~ on in spite of the weather.*

come round, (a) ~ by a circuitous route: *The road was blocked so we had to ~ round by the fields.* (b) pay an informal visit to: *Won't you ~ round and see me some time?*

fall through, fail; miscarry; come to nothing: *His scheme fell through.*

look after sb/sth, (a) take care of; watch over; attend to: *Who will ~ after the children while their mother is in hospital? He needs someone to ~ after him. He's well able to ~ after himself/to ~ after his own interests.*

make sth up, (a) complete: *We still need £5 to ~ up the sum we asked for. They need ten more men to ~ up their full complement.* (b) supply; ~ good: *Our losses have to be made up with more loans.* (c) invent; compose (esp to deceive): *The whole story is made up. It's all a made-up story. Stop making things up!*

pull sth down, destroy or demolish, eg an old building. **pull sb down,** (of illness, etc) weaken;

put off, (of a boat or crew) leave: *We put off from the pier.* **put sth off,** (a) postpone: *put off a meeting; put off going to the dentist.*

Has the house been put up for auction? **a put-up job,** sth done in order to give a false impression, to swindle sb, etc. **put sb up,** provide lodging and food (for): *We can put you up for the weekend.*

take after sb, resemble (esp a parent or relation) in features or character: *Your daughter does not ~ after you in any way.*

take off, (a) make a start in jumping. (b) (of an air-craft) leave the ground and rise: *The plane took off despite the fog.* ~ **sth off,** (a) remove: *~ off one's shirt. Why don't you ~ (= shave) off that silly little moustache? The surgeon took off (= amputated) his leg.*

Please try me for the job, let me do it as an experiment. ⇨ trial(1). [VP15B] **try sth on,** (a) put on (a garment, show, etc) to see whether it fits, looks well, etc: *I want to try the shoes on before I buy them.* (b) (colloq) make a bold or impudent attempt.

2 Look at this entry for the phrasal verb 'bring sb/sth up'.

> **bring sb/sth up**, (a) educate; rear: *She has brought up five children. If children are badly brought up they behave badly.* (b) vomit: *~ up one's dinner.* (c) call attention to: *These are facts that can always be brought up against you*, used as evidence against you. *These are matters that you can ~ up in committee.* (d) (mil) summon to the front line: *We need to ~ up more tanks.* (e) *~ for trial: He was brought up on a charge of drunken driving.* (f) cause to stop suddenly: *His remarks brought me up short/sharp/with a jerk.*

Which use of **bring up** is in these sentences, (a), (b), (c), (d), (e) or (f)

I thought you brought up a very interesting point at the end of the lecture.
Her mother died in childbirth and she was brought up by her father.
The war is going badly. We need to bring up more soldiers.
The journey was so bumpy that the baby couldn't help bringing up her breakfast.

3 Replace the words in italics with one of the phrasal verbs on pages 68 and 69.

a. They're going to *demolish* this building soon and put up a supermarket.

b. He*'s like* his father in many ways. They're both gentle, soft-spoken men.

c. I'll have to *postpone* the trip. Next weekend would be a dreadful time to go.

d. She *didn't stop* eating the sweets until they were all gone.

e. Don't worry about a hotel. Some friends of mine will *give you a bed* for the night.

f. *Taking care of* children can be a demanding job.

g. I've tried to *educate* my children to be quite independent.

h. His plans to make a fortune *didn't work* because he didn't have the first idea about business.

i. Don't worry. The bomb won't *explode*.

j. You didn't believe what he said, did you? He *invented* the whole story from start to finish.

Listening

Pre-listening task

1 Talk to another student. What do you know about these places?

The Himalayas
Bangladesh
The Sudan
The Amazon jungle

2 **T.34** You're going to hear an interview with David Attenborough.
Here is the introduction.

'David Attenborough knows the world better than most people. He's spent much of the last seven years globe-trotting for his hugely successful television programmes *Life on Earth* and *The Living Planet*.
But his next series might well be named *The End of Life on the Dying Planet*. David Attenborough is very gloomy about much of what he's seen.'

David Attenborough talks about the places mentioned on page 69. What do you think is happening in these places that makes him 'gloomy'?

Listening for gist

Listen to the interview.
What *is* making David Attenborough gloomy about each place?
Is there a common cause?

Comprehension check

1 Why are forests cut down in the Himalayas?
2 'The trees were umbrellas.' What does this mean?
3 What happens to the soil without trees?
4 How are floods caused in Bangladesh?
5 What is the 'devastating statistic' about the desert in the Sudan?
6 Why does David Attenborough call it a 'heart-breaking' statistic?
7 Why did he not believe at first that the Amazon jungle could disappear?
8 How are statistics about the disappearing jungle made?
9 How much jungle is being destroyed every year?
10 Why are the plants in tropical rain forests important to us?

What do you think?

1 David Attenborough's last words in the interview are 'They are coming our way.'
What do you understand by this?

2 What are some of the future possibilities that David Attenborough is afraid of?

Example
There might be no more tropical plants.

Speaking

Discussion

Are you a pessimist or an optimist? Answer these questions for yourself, and discuss them with other students.

About you Do you think . . .

1 your life will be similar in the future to what it has been up to now?
   a. ☐ Yes.
   b. ☐ No. It will change a lot.
   c. ☐ No. It will change a little.

2 your standard of living will
   a. ☐ get better?
   b. ☐ get worse?
   c. ☐ stay the same?

3 you will
   a. ☐ stay in the same job?
   b. ☐ find a job that really satisfies you?
   c. ☐ live to work or work to live?

4 your children will have a
   a. ☐ better
   b. ☐ easier
   c. ☐ more comfortable
   d. ☐ more dangerous
   childhood than you did?

About the world Do you think . . .

1 that as we learn more, we are becoming more tolerant of people of different
   a. ☐ nationalities?
   b. ☐ religions?
   c. ☐ colours?

2 many species of animals will become extinct? Which?

3 we will find new sources of energy that are
   a. ☐ efficient?
   b. ☐ cheap?
   c. ☐ safe?

4 we are becoming
   a. ☐ wiser?
   b. ☐ more selfish?
   c. ☐ more materialistic?
   d. ☐ more nationalistic?

Writing

Sentence combination

Re-write these sentences to produce a coherent paragraph.

Example
Bert Langley is a fireman.
He is 38.
He lives in Dover.
He had a shock yesterday.
Bert Langley, a 38-year-old fireman from Dover, had a shock yesterday.

David Attenborough is a naturalist.
David Attenborough has been travelling the world for seven years.
David Attenborough has produced a lot of television documentaries.
The television documentaries have been shown in 37 countries.
David Attenborough is very worried about our world.
He is depressed by what human beings are doing to our world.

Human beings are cutting down too many trees.
Human beings need firewood to cook.
Human beings need firewood to keep themselves warm.
Trees are being cut down all over the world.
Areas of forests the size of Scotland disappear every year.
Trees are like umbrellas.
Trees protect good soil.
Rain washes away good soil.
Good soil becomes desert.
People cannot grow crops.

David Attenborough believes people in the West are short-sighted.
Governments are spending some money on conservation.
This money is not enough.
David Attenborough believes all people will suffer from the lack of trees.
The trees and forests can never be replaced.

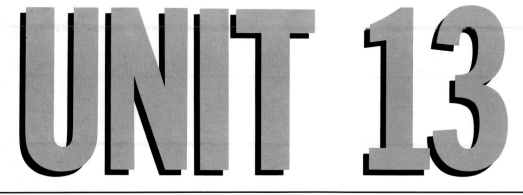

UNIT 13

The Passive

In the red

PRESENTATION

BROUGHTOR FINANCE LTD

23, Harbott Rd. London W4

Mrs G Ramoun   23 November 1985
6 Petal Road
London W3

Dear Madam

                        Balance   Credit limit

Re: Account No. 07456 222 489   £567 Debit   £450

It is with regret that we now give you formal notice that your account
has been closed. Your credit limit has been exceeded by over £100.
Customers are asked to apply in writing if they wish their credit
to be extended, and this was not done. You were warned last month that
this would be the result. In accordance with the conditions of use,
a copy of which has already been sent to you, the whole of the balance
is payable with immediate effect.

You are required to return to us your credit card, but before doing so
it should be cut in half for security.

A pre-addressed envelope (not pre-paid) is enclosed.

Yours faithfully

R. J. Box

R J Box
General Manager

● Grammar questions

Underline the examples of the *passive* in this letter.
Why is the passive used?
Change the passive sentences into the active.

PRACTICE

1 The passive is often used in formal situations. Work in pairs. Find and discuss other aspects of the letter that make it formal and distant. What would be the more informal, spoken form?

Example
Written *It is with regret...*
Spoken *We are sorry...*

Written *we now give you formal notice...*
Spoken *we have to tell you...*

2 Turn these newspaper headlines into radio news headlines.

Example
Escaped prisoner recaptured
The prisoner who escaped from prison two days ago has been recaptured.

a **Hijacked jet blown up**

b **Cure for cancer at last**

c **7 Pickets arrested in miners' strike**

d **40 killed in train crash in Sweden**

e ## Astronauts rescued in daring adventure

Now continue the stories briefly.

3 Here are the opening lines of six different stories.
Discuss why the active or passive has been used. What is the *main focus* of the sentence?
Continue the stories briefly to show where the main focus is.

a. Vauxhall cars are made in Birmingham and Bristol. They have a reputation. . .

b. The workers who are on strike in Birmingham and Bristol make Vauxhall cars.

c. A 70-year-old pensioner, Mrs Gladys Parker, yesterday found a puma in her back garden.

d. Roman ruins were found yesterday in the back garden of a pensioner.

e. Vincent van Gogh painted his pictures with the utmost care.

f. 'Sunflowers' was painted towards the end of van Gogh's life.

4 **T.35** Listen to this man and woman talking. She is telling him about a newspaper article she read. She uses the active more often than the passive.
Complete these sentences as you think they appeared in the newspaper article.

Toothache may bite the dust

TOOTHACHE could be a thing of the past within a few years. A possible cure _____ doctors at Guy's Hospital, London.
Toothache _____ an excess of sugar in our diet. The sugar _____ _____ by bacteria that are found in the mouth, and it is these acids that attack the teeth and make cavities. Researchers have discovered a vaccine that attacks the bacteria. Tests _____ on monkeys to establish its reliability and safety. The new vaccine _____ _____ all children when they reach the age of three.

● Language review

The passive: Use
Passive sentences move the focus of a sentence from the subject to the object of an *active* sentence.
Help! My wallet's been stolen.
Arrest that man! He's stolen my wallet.
The rules of use are exactly the same as for the *active.*
Letters are delivered twice a day.
(*Present Simple* for habit.)
The telephone was invented in 1876.
(*Past Simple* for a completed action.)

Translate
Champagne is produced in France.

_____

Two people were killed last night.

_____

Oil has been found in the Antarctic.

_____

This exercise must be done carefully.

◄ **Look back** at page 72 and underline the examples of the passive.

► **Grammar reference:** page 99.

SKILLS DEVELOPMENT

● Reading

Pre-reading task

1 Think of as many places as you can where computers are used to store and find information.

Example
banks/hotels/government offices/medical practices

2 Does the thought that such places might have records about *you*
a. worry you?
b. make you feel secure?
c. not bother you at all?

3 Look quickly at the article. How would the writer answer question 2?

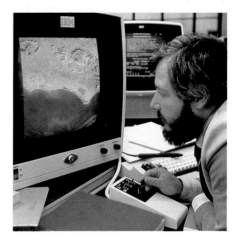

Carmen to read for w/b 7/9/99 (handwritten)

What price privacy? You could lose a job, a home, a loan through the contents of a file you may never see. Peter Freedman reports.

Someone Somewhere has you taped

Can you keep a SECRET? (handwritten)

Calman (signature on cartoon)

An American computer expert was approached recently by a British magazine asking her to track down details of all Lady Diana Spencer's credit card spendings in the period before the royal engagement. Though the magazine would not meet her asking fee, she said that technically the request was perfectly possible.

The contents of a file kept about you could stop you getting a job, a home, a loan. They could be unfair, or just plain inaccurate. But you'll never know, until something goes wrong in your life—you get turned down for a job, a mortgage, you are refused a credit card, and can't understand why—and only then, if you're lucky. Technology has made it possible to collect, store and retrieve almost limitless amounts of personal information about every aspect of our lives.

If you were ever in trouble at college or school; ever at the wrong end of a sacking (even if you knew it was an unfair one) or dealings with the police; ever failed to pay off a hire purchase agreement (even if it was because the goods were faulty); or have ever seen a psychiatrist—all this information is likely to be on record somewhere. On record, and, in our increasingly technological times, more accessible than ever to third parties who may use it as evidence against you.

But I've got nothing to hide . . .

The fact that you've got nothing to hide doesn't mean you've got nothing to worry about, because the information on record about you could quite simply be wrong. As it was about Jan Martin, a young woman film-maker turned down for a job after wrong information on a police computer was disclosed to a would-be employer. She and her husband had been travelling innocently in Holland shortly after the time of a Baader-Meinhoff terrorist incident, when someone wrongly identified him as a member of the gang and reported their car, registered in her name. When her 'terrorist links' were disclosed to her prospective employers, they understandably shied away. It was only because her father was a former senior policeman that he was able to discover the reason.

Whose file is it anyway?

Apart from the files of credit reference agencies, you have no legal right to see files kept about you. Even when you have strong reason to believe a file contains wrong information, you have no right to check it.

Employers, often hiring private detectives, seem to find it extraordinarily easy to discover almost all they need to know about you. Helena Kennedy explains, 'Policemen who leave the force often become private detectives but still have friends in the force who can get them information.' *The Observer* newspaper recently showed how easy it is, given a suitable story and a smattering of jargon, to obtain information by bluff from police computers. Computer freaks, whose hobby is breaking into official systems, don't even need to use the phone.

Computers do not alter the fundamental issues. But they do multiply the risks. They allow more data to be collected on more aspects of our lives, and increase both its rapid retrievability and the likelihood of its unauthorized transfer from one agency which might have a legitimate interest in it, to another which does not. Modern computer capabilities also raise the issue of what is known in the jargon as 'total data linkage'— the ability, by pressing a few buttons and waiting as little as a minute, to collate all the information about us held on all the major government and business computers into an instant dossier on any aspect of our lives.

Machine-readable passports

A recent *New Scientist* article reported that within five years most Western countries will be issuing their citizens with a machine-readable passport that will carry with it the threat of global surveillance of innocent travellers. Says journalist Steve Connor, 'The new passport could mean that anyone (crossing a border) can be stopped and checked until a computer statement of 'No trace' allows them to go on about their business. The computerised passport allows the list of people who, for various reasons, are labelled as suspicious, to expand almost without limit.'

Reading for specific information

Now read the article opposite, which appeared in a popular magazine.

Comprehension check

1 What did the magazine want to know about Princess Diana?
2 When, according to paragraph 2, will you find out about your file?
3 What sort of information might be on your file?
4 What happened to Jan Martin?
5 Why can't you check the information on your file?
6 What did *The Observer* newspaper do?
7 What is total data linkage?
8 What is the threat that the writer sees in machine-readable passports?

What do you think?

1 Is your answer to question 2 on page 73 the same *after* reading the article?
2 The writer is worried that *third parties* might use information against you.
a. What third parties does he mention?
b. Can you think of any other third parties that might use information against you?
3 Do you think the writer is right or wrong to be worried about machine-readable passports?
4 Would you describe the article as
a. balanced?
b. rightly concerned about individual liberty?
c. basically convincing but a little extreme?
d. over-reacting to something that isn't very important?
5 Think of some arguments in defence of the existence of such files.

Vocabulary

Guessing unknown words

Find these words in the article about computers. Study the context carefully and try to work out the meaning. Remember it is not always necessary to know the meaning of a word 100% – sometimes 50% is enough.

Paragraph 1 to track down

Paragraph 2 a loan/inaccurate/get turned down for . . . a mortgage/limitless

Paragraph 3 at the wrong end of a sacking/the goods were faulty

Paragraph 4 A would-be employer

Paragraph 6 the force *check next week.*

Opposites

In the second paragraph of the article about computers, there are two adjectives with negative prefixes.
Can you find them?
Negative prefixes un-/in-/im-/dis-

What is the opposite of these words? Use one of the *prefixes*.
If there is another word that has approximately the same meaning, write that too.

Word	Opposite	Similar meaning
safe	unsafe	dangerous
kind		
modest	- im	
happy		
complete		
expensive		
interesting		
important		
perfect		
friendly		
polite	im	
correct	in	
honest	disho	
certain	un	
flexible	in	

Speaking

The role of computers

– Did you know that there will soon be computers that can in a few seconds exchange more words than have ever been spoken in the whole history of mankind!
– Did you know that the age of the average computer programmer is 12?
– Did you know that if the car industry had developed at the same rate as the computer over the past few years, a Rolls-Royce would now cost 50p?

'With this new computerised machinery we can have more of our men playing cards than ever before'.

'I fed all your symptoms into the computer, Mr Bilkins, and it died'.

1 Work in groups.
Think of the advantages and disadvantages of computers in the world today, and any interest points.

Example

Advantage *Computers can do many very boring jobs very quickly and accurately.*

Disadvantage *They have caused a lot of unemployment.*

Interest point *Some people might not like them, but they are here to stay.*

Listening

Pre-listening task

1 How long does it take you to get to work?
2 Would you like to work at home? Or would you miss your colleagues and the social side of work?

Listening for gist

T.36 Listen to this interview with Lynn Dermott, who works for the Low Pay Unit. This is a voluntary organisation which monitors the effects of government policy and union action on the worst-paid members of the work force. She talks about possible future trends in working conditions. Computers and the development of the communications industry could mean that many people will work at home. On a separate piece of paper, list the advantages that she sees in this, and then reasons why she is afraid of such a development.

What do you think?

1 What in your opinion are the main advantages and disadvantages of working at home?
2 Could you do your job at home if you had the right equipment?
3 People say that soon we will do our shopping by computer from home, and that we will even be able to consult the doctor from home.
If telephones had television screens with them, how many jobs could be performed from home? teaching?/selling?/accountancy?/designing?

Writing

Linking words

Here is an informal letter with ten gaps.
Fill each gap with one of the following linking words or phrases.

fortunately/so/which/in my opinion/ anyway/as/actually/but/at the moment/personally

Dear Pam,

Thank you for your letter. I was astonished to hear about Sheila and David. I thought they were very happy together. ① _____ when I last saw them they were talking about having another baby, ② _____ quite surprised me ③ _____ they've already got four. I feel very sorry for Sheila, but ④ _____ I never liked David — too much of an intellectual.
⑤ _____, you'll be pleased to hear that Joey passed her driving test first time. ⑥ _____, she shouldn't be allowed on the road at all — she's far too careless and easily distracted.
We're having the living room decorated ⑦ _____, so the whole house is in a mess. ⑧ _____, it'll be finished before the weekend, because we've got Peter's parents coming to stay, ⑨ ___ I'll be busy cleaning and cooking as usual. They're no trouble, ⑩ ___ it would be nice to have a quiet weekend for a change.
Well, I must end now. Say hello to the family. Write again soon,

Angela.

UNIT 14

Reported statements

PRESENTATION

Joe applied for a job as junior clerk working for Frazier Products Limited. He got the job after an interview.

This is what the interviewer told him about the company:

Frazier Products Limited

— exports abroad
— has branches in America
— expanding company
— started in 1960
— employs 1,600 people
— introduced computers in 1983

This is what the interviewer told him about the job:

Junior Clerk

— pay rise after six months
— prospects of promotion
— subsidised canteen
— friendly staff
— sports facilities—squash, tennis, football

1 What were the interviewer's actual words?
Frazier Products Limited exports abroad.
You'll get a pay rise after six months.

2 After six months in the company Joe was very unhappy.
Everything that the interviewer had said was wrong.
Joe went to speak to the interviewer. Finish his comments about the company using, *'say'* or *'tell'*.

Example
You said/You told me the company exported abroad. It's not true!

3 Do the same for Joe's comments about the job, using:
'You said ...'; 'You told me ...'; 'I thought ...'; 'I hoped ...'

Example
I hoped I'd get a pay rise after six months.

Can you add to Joe's list of complaints?

● Grammar question

What is the basic rule in *reported speech*?

77

PRACTICE

In pairs perform a similar dialogue at a travel agent's.

Student A You have just come back from a disastrous holiday. All of the travel agent's promises were broken. Complain.

Student B You are the travel agent. Listen to A's complaints and make excuses and/or apologies.

Reported commands

PRESENTATION

Conflict

SHIPBUILDERS' STRIKE CONTINUES

Government takes action

The bitter strike over pay and redundancies has now lasted over 8 weeks. Shipbuilders have told their leaders to 'fight to the end' to stop dockyards from closing and 2,000 of their men losing their jobs.

Sir Albert Pringle, chairman of British Shipbuilders, has asked Peter Arkwright, the president of the Shipbuilders' Union, to attend a meeting next Thursday.

Meanwhile, the Government has ordered Sir Albert to give important naval contracts to the Japanese.

● Grammar question

– Underline the three *reported commands* in this newspaper article.
– What is the difference between *tell* in *reported statements* and *tell* in *reported commands*?

PRACTICE

1 Match the verbs with the following direct speech by putting the appropriate letters into the boxes.

1 ☐ ask   5 ☐ remind
2 ☐ tell   6 ☐ invite
3 ☐ warn   7 ☐ persuade
4 ☐ urge   8 ☐ advise

a. 'I think you should accept the pay rise,' Sir Albert Pringle said to the shipbuilders' leader.

b. 'We really must stay united,' Peter Arkwright said to his members.

c. 'Don't forget to come to the meeting,' Sir Albert said to his secretary.

d. 'Be careful of the press. They often make mistakes,' said a colleague to Peter Arkwright.

e. 'I think we should return to work,' said Peter. 'Well, if you think it's a good idea, we agree,' said the shipbuilders.

f. 'Please reconsider this offer,' Sir Albert said to Mr Arkwright.

g. 'Stop work!' Peter Arkwright said to the shipbuilders.

h. 'Have lunch with me,' said Sir Albert to Peter.

2 Put the sentences **a/h** into indirect speech, using the verbs from numbers **1–8**.

Example
Sir Albert Pringle advised the shipbuilders' leader to accept the pay rise.

3 Divide into two groups.
| T.37 | You are each going to listen to a short tape.

Group A You are going to listen to Sir Albert Pringle, the chairman of British Shipbuilders, giving his views on the strike.

Group B You are going to listen to Peter Arkwright, the president of the Shipbuilders' Union, giving his views on the strike.

After listening, pair up with a student from the other group. Compare what you heard like this.
Sir Albert Pringle said he thought the strike was a waste of time. Peter Arkwright said the shipbuilders' jobs were in danger.

Reported questions

PRESENTATION

The car accident

| T.38 | A policeman is giving evidence in court.
PC Jones I asked Mr Walter where he was going, and he told me he was looking for a hotel.
Solicitor But there aren't any hotels around there.
PC Jones That's right. Then I asked him if he knew the area, but he said he didn't.
Solicitor I see.

● Grammar questions

– What was the conversion between PC Jones and Mr Walter?

Begin like this.
PC Jones *Where . . .?*

– How are questions reported?
– What's the difference between *ask* in reported commands and *ask* in reported questions?

PRACTICE

1 Report PC Jones's other questions.

'What's your name?'
He asked me _____

'Where have you come from?'
He asked me _____

79

'When did you pass your test?'
He asked me _____

'How old are you?'
He asked me _____

'Where do you live?'
He asked me _____

'Why aren't you wearing a seat belt?'
He asked me _____

'Is this your car?'
He asked me *if it was my car.*
or
. . . *whether it was my car.*

'Is the car insured?'
He asked me _____

'Have you had it long?'
He asked me _____

'Do you often use this road?'
He asked me _____

'Are you aware you have a flat tyre?'
He asked me _____

2   Look at this newspaper headline.

BANK ROBBERS ESCAPE IN STOLEN CAR

Speak about the headlines like this:
I wonder how much they stole.
I don't know where the robbery happened.
I'd like to know if anyone was hurt.

Do the same for these headlines.

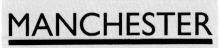

MANCHESTER MAN WINS FORTUNE

EARTHQUAKE HORROR

Prime Minister to see U.S. President

ROYAL SCANDAL

Runaway children go back to family

Reported statements

The normal rule is **one tense back**.
'I'm going.' *He said he was going.*
'She's passed her exam.' *He told me she had passed her exam.*
This also applies to reported thoughts.
'She'll come on Thursday.' *I thought she would come on Thursday.*

Translate

He said he was going

He told me she had passed her exam.

Reported commands

These are introduced by verbs such as **ask**, **tell**, and **persuade**.
He asked me to come and see him.
She told me to work harder.

Translate

He asked me to wait.

She told me to work harder.

Reported questions

In reported and indirect questions, the word order is the same as the answer.
Answer: *Peter lives in Bournemouth.*

He asked me	
I wonder	*where Peter lives.*
I don't know	

As in reported speech, the normal rule is **one tense back**.
'What are you doing here?'
He asked me what I was doing there.

Translate

He asked me what I wanted to do.

She asked me if I would like a drink.

I wonder why they were going so early

◀ **Look back** at page 79 and underline the examples of *reported questions*.

▶ **Grammar reference:** page 100.

SKILLS DEVELOPMENT

Vocabulary

Ways of speaking

1 Here are some words which describe the way we talk. Look them up in your dictionary, and write a short sentence in direct speech to illustrate the meaning.

Example
to scream *'Look out! The lion's going to jump!'* she screamed.

to whisper	to moan
to stammer	to gasp
to mumble	to yell
to swear	to boast
to grumble	to sigh

Work in pairs.
Say out loud some of the sentences you've written in an appropriate manner. Don't say the verb (e.g. *to scream*). Can your partner guess the right verb?

2 A text often uses an adverb to describe the way something is spoken.

Do the same for these.
. . . she said angrily.
. . . he said proudly.
. . . she said sarcastically.
. . . he said shyly.
. . . she said tactfully.
. . . she said apologetically.
. . . he said hesitatingly.
. . . she said wittily.
. . . he said cheerfully.
. . . he said selfishly.

Speaking

Pairwork

Think of a story that is currently in the news. It could be about politics, sport, personalities, anything.

Student A   You are one of the people involved in this news story. Decide who you are.
You are going to be interviewed by a reporter. Make sure you know the general background to the story and who the other people involved are. You will also be asked about possible future developments, so you might have to use your imagination.

Student B   You are a reporter. You are going to interview A who is involved in this news story. Prepare your questions.
You want to know about past events, what is happening now, possible future developments.
Do you want to know anything about other people involved?

When you are ready, conduct the interview.
After the interview, work together to write the news report.

Reading

Comparing newspaper styles

1 The Kennedy family is one of America's most famous families. Briefly discuss what you know about them.

2 This is how three different newspapers treated the same story in April 1984.
The newspapers are *The Guardian*, The *Daily Mirror* and *The Sun*.

The Guardian is considered to be a 'quality' newspaper, and reports stories quite factually.
The *Daily Mirror* and *The Sun* are popular papers, and tend to report stories dramatically with colourful language.

3 Read the three articles carefully and compare them. Consider the following:
– Length of the article
– Visual presentation

– Information included or excluded
– The order of the information
– Language style

Example
murdered v. assassinated
Mum, Ethel v. his mother Mrs Ethel Kennedy

– Amount of detail
Example
room 107

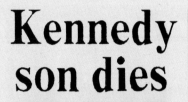

David Kennedy

From Alex Brummer in Washington

David Kennedy, aged 28, the fourth son of the late Robert Kennedy, was yesterday found dead in an hotel room in Palm Beach, Florida, where he had been visiting his ailing grandmother, Mrs Rose Kennedy.

The latest tragedy to strike the Kennedy family came to its most vulnerable member. In a recent biography, David Kennedy, who had a long history of drug problems, was described as the most self-destructive child of the two assassinated Kennedy brothers.

The death was announced in a statement from the offices of Senator Edward Kennedy on Capitol Hill.

The West Palm Beach police chief offered no immediate comment on whether the death was drug related.

EDWARD KENNEDY'S TRIBUTE:

❛ We all pray that David has finally found the peace that he did not find in life ❜

KENNEDY BOY DRUGS DEATH

Bobby's tragic son
is found in hotel room

From MARTIN DUNN in New York

MURDERED Senator Bobby Kennedy's son David was found dead last night after years of drug abuse.

David, 28-year-old nephew of assassinated President John F. Kennedy, was discovered in a hotel room in Florida's fashionable Palm Beach resort.

Police, alerted by hotel receptionist Betty Barnett, rushed to the scene and immediately cordoned off the building.

Mrs Barnett made the horrific find in room 107 after David's worried mother Ethel called the hotel from Boston.

Mrs Kennedy was

Mum Ethel . . . anxious phone call

THE KENNEDY CURSE
—See Centre Pages

alarmed because she had been unable to contact her son for more than 24 hours.

She had been expecting fair-haired David to fly home early yesterday.

David's death is the latest tragedy in the history of America's "first family."

In November, 1963, President John was assassinated in Dallas.

In June, 1968, David's father Bobby was gunned down in Los Angeles.

In 1973 Senator Ed-

ward's son Teddy had a leg amputated because of bone cancer.

David's uncle Edward, whose own career crashed when he was accused of letting a girl drown in a car crash, said last night:

❛ With trust in God, we all pray that David has finally found the peace that he did not find in life ❜

He added: "This is a

Continued on Centre Pages

David Kennedy . . . he fought a losing battle against drug addiction

£40,000 BINGO! TODAY'S LUCKY NUMBERS—See Page 23

BOBBY: Assassinated

BOBBY KENNEDY'S SON FOUND DEAD

DAVID: Drug addict

Rachel was the love of his life

BRITISH actress Rachel Ward befriended David Kennedy after meeting him in a nightclub.

Later David described the Thorn Birds actress as "the most beautiful girl in the world".

According to a recent article in Playboy magazine, Rachel and David had an affair.

David told his friends she had no idea he used drugs.

"I was back on 'smack' (heroin)," he said. "She had no idea of what I was up to.

"I don't know what she thought of all those little marks on my arms when I was naked. I guess she thought they were some odd Kennedy rash."

Rachel once went to South America with him, and she said afterwards he gave no sign of being on drugs.

After they split, she started going out with folk singer Art Garfunkel.

She married Australian actor Bryan Brown, who played her husband in the Thorn Birds, last year.

FRIEND: Thornbirds star Rachel Ward went to South America with David and said later: "He's not the pathetic character he is made out to be".

DAVID KENNEDY, who turned to drugs after his father Robert was assassinated, was found dead yesterday on the floor of his hotel room.

His body was discovered by an hotel receptionist alerted by his mother, who was waiting by the phone for news of him.

David, the 28-year-old third son of Robert and Ethel Kennedy, had been having treatment for drug problems and had suffered from a heart disease which may have been brought on by drugs.

But police refused to say last night whether drugs had caused his death.

Difficult

"We have no evidence at this time of any drug use," said Joseph Terlizzese, police chief of Palm Beach, the Florida resort where David died.

David's uncle, Senator Edward Kennedy, was last night on his way to Florida from Washington to find out details of his death.

In a statement, Senator Kennedy said:

❝This is a very difficult time for all the members of our family, including David's mother, Ethel, and his brothers and sisters who tried to help him.

All of us loved him very much. With

From DAVID BRADBURY in New York

trust in God, we all pray that David has finally found the peace that he did not find in life.

David checked into the £80-a-night luxury hotel last Friday.

Receptionist Betty Barnett found him dead after his mother phoned from Boston.

Miss Barnett said last night: "Mrs. Kennedy told me that David had not been seen for the past 24 hours, that she had not heard from him and that he was due to fly to Boston today.

"She asked whether I would check the room and see if his clothes had been packed.

"I went in and was shocked to find David lying dead on his bed."

She then went back to the phone to say her that David was just lying there and that ambulance men had been called. Mrs Kennedy asked to be phoned back with further news.

The ambulance men arrived and tried to revive David with electric shock treatment. But a few minutes later, hotel manager Dennis Heffernan phoned Mrs. Kennedy to tell her that her son was dead.

● Curse of the Kennedys — See Page 3

Listening

T.39 Listen to this interview with Mrs Jane Simpson, a London divorce lawyer.

In the interview she talks about the following topics.

- Who most often wants the divorce, the husband or wife.
- The most common reason for divorce.
- Reasons why marriages break down.
- How to make marriages work.
- Is is too easy to get divorced?
- Should children be a reason for a couple staying together?

Before listening, discuss these topics and questions with a partner.
- What do you think the answers are?
- What is your opinion?
After listening, compare your answers with Mrs Simpson's.

Comprehension check

1 What, according to Mrs Simpson, are the two real main reasons for divorce?
2 What are the more specific reasons given from the woman's point of view?
  And from the man's?
3 Why does she say that adultery is often a *symptom* of a marriage breaking down, and not a reason for it to break down?
4 What is her advice to people who have recently got divorced?
5 What would she like to change in the divorce laws?
6 What does she think of her job?

What do you think?

1 Is it possible to get divorced in your country?
  Are the laws generally liked?
  Would you like them to change?
2 Approximately one in three marriages in Britain ends in divorce.
  Do you think it should be more difficult to get divorced?
  Do you think it should be more difficult to get married?
3 'Marriage should be a five-year renewable contract, not a life-long commitment.'
  What do you think of this proposition?

Writing

Presenting both sides of an argument

Read this text about the advantages and disadvantages of sharing a flat.

1 How is the text organised? What is the purpose of each paragraph?

2 Which of the words underlined could be replaced by one of the following?
On the other hand/In my opinion/ First of all/Especially/Moreover/ Another point is that

3 Look at the beginning of paragraph 2.
... sharing a flat has some distinct disadvantages.
... sharing a flat does have some distinct disadvantages.
What is the difference?

4 'What happens if you want to go to bed but your flat-mate wants to play music?'
This is called a rhetorical question, because the writer either knows the answer, or he doesn't want the answer. He is simply making a point in his argument.

5 Write short paragraphs discussing the advantages and disadvantages of the following. Conclude with your own preferences.
- Being self-employed or an employee.
- Holidays in your own country or holidays abroad.
- Living in a town or in the country.
- Learning English in a school or learning English while you're doing a job in an English-speaking country.

Sharing a flat certainly has some advantages. <u>To begin with</u>, it should be cheaper, and if you are sharing with people that you get on well with, it is nice to have some company at home rather than being all on your own. <u>Also</u> the household chores are shared, and that is very important. <u>Particularly</u> when you are younger, and you are living apart from your parents for the first time, it can be very enjoyable to live with people of your own age, whose interests and life-style you share.

<u>However</u>, sharing a flat does have some distinct disadvantages, and the main one is that the flat is not your own, so you cannot do what you want in it. What happens if you want to go to bed but your flat-mate wants to play music? To a certain extent you have to be unselfish. <u>What is more</u>, there can be little privacy.

<u>I would say that</u> as you get older, it is probably better to live on your own. Having had my own flat for a few years, I would not like to have to share again.

85

Grammar section

UNIT 1
The Present

The Present Simple (1)

I come to work by bus.
He works in a bank.

Form

Positive

I	
You	
We	work in a bank.
They	

There are no changes to the base form of the verb.

He	
She	works in a bank.
It	

The 3rd person singular adds -s to the base form of the verb.

Negative

I	
You	
We	**don't** work every day.
They	

Put **don't (do not)** in front of the base form of the verb.

He	
She	**doesn't** work every day.
It	

Put **doesn't (does not)** in front of the base form of the verb in the 3rd person singular.

Question

	I	
	you	
Where **do**	we	work?
	they	

Put **do** in front of the subject.

	he	
Where **does**	she	work?
	it	

Put **does** in front of the subject in the 3rd person singular.

Short answers:
A *Do you work in a bank?*
B *Yes, I do.*

A *Does she speak French?*
B *No, she doesn't.*

Use

1 It is used to express an action which happens again and again, that is, a *habit*.

   He smokes twenty cigarettes a day.
   We go to the country every weekend.

2 It is used to express a fact that stays the same for a long time, that is, a *state*.

   We live in Oxford.
   He works in a bank.

3 It is used to express something which is *always true* about a person or about the world.

   She comes from Spain.
   I speak three languages.
   The sun rises in the east.
   It rains a lot in Britain.
   Water boils at 100° centigrade.

Notes

1 **Adverbs of frequency**
   The *Present Simple* is often found with adverbs of frequency. They are listed here according to the approximate degree of frequency that they express.

always	100%
usually	
often	
sometimes	50%
not often	
rarely	
never	0%

   Look at the position of these adverbs.

   I always get up at 7.00.
   We sometimes go sailing at weekends.
   Do you often go to the cinema?

The adverb comes between the subject and the main verb. Be careful with the verb **to be**, which comes before the adverb.

I am always late for school.
He's never at home when I call.

2 **The spelling of the 3rd person singular.**
a. The normal rule is add **-s** to the base form of the verb.
   wants/eats/helps/drives
b. Add **-es** to verbs that end in **-ss -sh -ch -x** and **-o**.
   he kisses/she washes/he watches/ she fixes/it goes
c. Verbs which end in a **consonant + y** change to **-ies**
   it carries/she hurries/he flies
   But verbs which end in a **vowel + y** are normal.
   she buys/he says

The Present Continuous

The baby's crying.
Where are you going?

Form

All continuous tenses are formed in the same way.

subject + verb **to be** + present
participle

For different tenses, change the tense of the verb **to be**.

Positive

I'm (I am)	
You're (You are)	
He's (He is)	
She's (She is)	working.
We're (We are)	
They're (They are)	

Where	am I	going?
	are you	
	is he	
	is she	
	are we	
	are they	

Negative

I'm not	going home.
You aren't	
He isn't	
She isn't	
We aren't	
They aren't	

Short answers:

A *Are you learning English?*
B *Yes, I am.*

A *Is Maria reading at the moment?*
B *No, she isn't.*

Note that we cannot say *Yes, I'm* or *Yes, she's*. This is WRONG.

Use

All continuous tenses have the idea of an *activity in progress*, and the activity is *temporary*.

I can't answer the phone. I'm having a bath.
Peter is a student, but he's working as a waiter during the holidays.

Compare these sentences with the same verbs in the *Present Simple*.

I have a bath twice a week. (a habit)
Anna works in a travel bureau. (a state)

1 The *Present Continuous* is often used to express an activity happening at the moment of speaking.

What's that smell? Something's burning.
Why are you wearing that funny hat?

2 It is also used to express an activity that is happening for a limited period at or near the present, but is not necessarily happening at the moment.

Please don't take that book. Anne's reading it.
Andrew's spending a lot of time in the library these days, as he's writing a book.

Notes

1 **The spelling of the present participle.**
a. The normal rule is add **-ing** to the base form of the verb.
going/wearing/visiting/eating
b. Verbs that end in one **-e** lose the **-e**.
smoking/coming/hoping/writing
c. Verbs that end in **-ee** keep the **-ee**.
*seeing/agreeing/(These have **double e**.)*
d. In verbs of one syllable, with one written vowel + one written consonant, the consonant is doubled.
stopping/hitting/running/planning/beginning/travelling

Exceptions
If the consonant is **y** or **w**, it is not doubled.
playing/showing

UNIT 2

The Present Simple (2)

For the form and uses of the *Present Simple*, see page 87.

There are certain groups of 'state' verbs that are almost never used in the *Present Continuous*. This is because, by definition, they have the idea of permanency.

I like Indian food.

It is not only in the present that I like Indian food, it is also in the past and the future.
So *I'm liking Indian food* is WRONG.

These are the groups of verbs.

1 **Verbs of the mind**
She **knows** a lot about astrology.
Do you **understand** what I'm saying?
What do you **think** of that book?
Other verbs like this are **believe/forget/remember/mean/doubt.**

2 **Verbs of emotion and feeling**
I **like** playing football.
They **love** listening to music.
I **hate** getting up in the morning.
Other verbs like this are **dislike/prefer/want/care.**

3 **Verbs of the five senses**
see/smell/taste/hear/touch
They are used with **can.**
I **can smell** something burning.
Can you **see** Peter?
What's that noise? **Can** your **hear** it?

4 **Verbs of possession**
I **have** two sisters.
He **owns** a Rolls Royce.
This book **belongs** to me.

5 **Certain other verbs**
A newspaper **costs** about 20p.
I **need** a bath.
Be careful. That bottle **contains** poison.
Other verbs are **depend/consist/seem.**

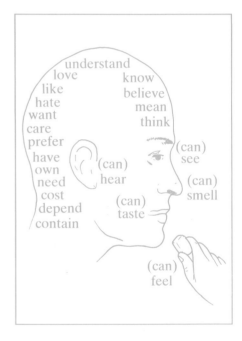

Notes

Some of these verbs can be used in the continuous form, but the meaning changes.

a. **Think**
When **to think** means **have the opinion**, it cannot be used in the continuous.
What do you think of classical music?
I think it's boring.

However, when **to think** means **to have** in one's thoughts, it can be used in the continuous, because it is a mental activity and not a state.

You aren't listening to me. What are you thinking about?

I'm thinking about a letter I received this morning.

b. **Have**
When **to have** means **possess**, it cannot be used in the continuous.
I have black hair.
I'm having black hair is WRONG.

When **to have** + **noun** implies an activity, it can be used in the continuous.
John's having a bath.
We're having lamb for lunch.

c. **See** and **look at**
Hear and **listen to**
See and **hear** as verbs of the senses cannot be used in the continuous, but **look at** and **listen to** can.

She's looking at my holiday photographs.

Don't turn the music off. I'm listening to it.

The difference is that we can *choose* to look or listen, so it requires active effort.

UNIT 3

The Past

Past Simple and Past Continuous

I went to Greece for my holidays last year.
We stayed for two weeks.

Form

Positive

I	
You	
She	worked hard.
We	
They	

There are no changes for the different persons.

Negative

I	
You	
He	didn't see anybody.
We	
They	

Put **didn't (did not)** before the base form of the verb.

Question

Did	you she we they	go by air?

Put **did** before the subject + the base form of the verb.

Short answers:
A *Did you speak to Peter?*
B *Yes, I did.*

A *Did the car start?*
B *No, it didn't.*

Use

1 The *Past Simple* expresses an action which happened at a specific time in the past and is now finished.
Look at some of the time expressions found with this tense.

I did it last year/last month/two years ago/two hours ago/yesterday morning/yesterday evening/in 1983/in summer/when I was young

2 The *Past Simple* is used to tell a story.

There was once a man who lived in a small house in the country. One day he left his house and went into town. On the way he met . . .

Notes

1 A lot of very common verbs are irregular in the *Past Simple* form.
go/come/went/came
There is a list of them on page 102.

2 The spelling of regular verbs.
a. The normal rule is add **-ed** to the base form of the verb.
worked/wanted/helped/washed

b. When verbs end in **-e**, just add **-d**.
baked/liked/used

c. In verbs of one syllable, with one written vowel + one written consonant, the consonant is doubled.

stopped/planned/grabbed

But *cooked/looked* (there are two vowels.)
The consonant is not doubled if it is **y** or **w**.
played/showed

d. In most two-syllabled verbs the consonant is doubled if the stress is on the second syllable.

pre'ferred/ad'mitted

But *'entered/'visited* (The stress is on the first syllable).

e. Verbs that end in a consonant + **y** change to **-ied**.
carried/buried

The Past Continuous

He was wearing a uniform.
The birds were singing.

Form

subject + **was/were** + present participle

Positive

I	
He	was going home.
She	

You	
We	were going home.
They	

Negative

I	
He	wasn't working.
She	

You	
We	weren't working.
They	

Question

Where was	I she it	going?

Where **were**	you we they	going?

Short answers:
A *Was she wearing a hat?*
B *Yes, she was.*

A *Were they going home?*
B *No, they weren't.*

For the spelling of the present participle, see page 88.

Use

As with all continuous tenses, there is the idea of *duration* and *activity in progress* over a period of time.

Compare these sentences.
a. *At 10.00 I had a bath.*
b. *At 10.00 I was having a bath.*

a. means I *began* to have a bath at 10.00.
b. means I was *already* in the bath at 10.00, the activity was in progress.

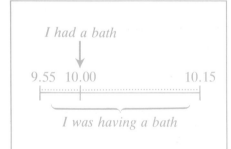

```
        I had a bath
             │
             ▼
9.55  10.00              10.15
  └──────┴──────────────────┘
      I was having a bath
```

1 Just as the *Present Continuous* is used to express an activity happening *now*, the *Past Continuous* is used to express an activity happening *at a particular time in the past*.

What were you doing at 8.00 last night? I was watching television.

When I got home the children were crying and the dog was barking.

2 Because of the idea of duration, the *Past Continuous* is used for *descriptions*.

This morning was really beautiful. The sun was shining, the birds were singing, and everyone in the street was smiling and saying hello to each other.

Maria looked beautiful last night. She was wearing a lovely velvet skirt.

90

3 The *Past Continuous* is also used to express *an activity that is interrupted*.
Compare these sentences:

When we arrived, she made some coffee.
– means she began making coffee *after* we arrived.

When we arrived, she was making some coffee.
– means she was *in the middle* of making coffee, and we interrupted her.

The action in brackets happened in the middle of the continuous activity described.

While I was having a bath (the phone rang.)

While I was walking in the park (it began to rain.)

He was crossing the road (when I saw him.)

The students were working (when the teacher walked in.)

4 The *Past Continuous* can express *incompleteness* when contrasted with the *Past Simple*.

I read a book yesterday (and finished it).

I was reading a book yesterday (and I'll finish it today).

UNIT 4
Asking People To Do Things

Introduction to modal verbs

Could, **would**, **will**, and **shall** are all modal verbs. They are sometimes called *modal auxiliaries*, because they are always used with another verb in its base form.

Could you come?
I'll help.

They are used to express requests:
Can you open the door, please?
Would you help me for a minute?

and also to express offers:
I'll carry your bags for you.
Shall I get you an aspirin?

Form

a. They do not add -s in the 3rd person singular.
She'll help you.
He can swim.
NOT *He cans swim.*

b. For the question, invert the subject and the modal verb.
Could you tell me the answer?
Can you swim?
NOT *Do you can swim?*

c. For the negative, add **not** or -**n't** to the modal.
You mustn't do that.
I can't see him.
or
I cannot see him. (**cannot** is *one* word)

NOT *I don't can see him.*

Exception
will not becomes **won't** in the short form and **shall not** becomes **shan't**.

Use

Modals have different meanings in different situations.

I can swim.
Can here expresses ability.

Can I go now?
Can here asks for permission.

Could you help me?
Could here is a request.

I could read when I was four.
Could here expresses ability.

Asking people to do things

Could Would Can Will	you help me, please?

All four modals can be used to ask someone to do something for you.

Can and **will** are more familiar.
Could you . . . ? is one of the most common forms, and is useful for foreign students as it is appropriate in many situations, both formal and informal.

For more uses of **could**, see Unit 10.
For more uses of **would**, see Unit 9.

Offering to do things

I'll help you with your homework.
In this unit **will** is used to express willingness to help. In spoken English it is always contracted to -ll.

Shall I get you something to drink?

In this unit **shall** is used in the question to express an offer. It is almost always used only in the 1st person, singular or plural. **Shall** can also express an invitation or a suggestion.

What shall we do tonight? Shall we go out or stay at home?

For more uses of **will** and **shall**, see Unit 5.

UNIT 5
Future Tenses (1)

Will

I think it will rain tomorrow.
I'll see you later.

Form

subject + **will/won't** + base form of verb

For an introduction to modal verbs, see page 90.

Positive

I He They	'll come on time.

Negative

I She You	won't be late.

Question

When **will**	I you they	arrive?

Use

In Unit 4, **will** was used to express *willingness*.

In this unit, **will** is used to express a *prediction* and an *intention*.

1 **Will** expressing *a future prediction*.
   I think it'll rain tomorrow.
   You'll feel better after you've taken this medicine.

   It is important to understand the difference between **will** as a modal verb, which expresses concepts such as willingness, intention, etc., and **will** as an auxiliary of the future, where, like all auxiliaries, it only shows *tense* and has no intrinsic meaning at all. **Will** for prediction merely signifies 'This is a future tense'. It is also called the 'future as fact', or the 'neutral future'.

   Here are some more examples.
   One day I'll die.
   You'll fall off if you're not careful.
   He'll be dead before he's 30.
   I'll be 26 next Tuesday.

2 **Will** expressing a *future intention*.
   I'll have a steak, please.
   I'll see you next week.

   In this sentence **will** expresses an intention or decision *made at the moment of speaking*, that is, not planned or premeditated. In many languages this idea is expressed in the present tense, because the decision to act and the act itself are so close in time.

   A *Can I ring you tonight?*
   B *Yes, I'll give you my number. It's 3871425.*

   The decision to give the number is made only one second before the actual giving of it, and **will** does not really refer to the future, but signifies a present intention. *I give you my number* is WRONG.

   According to the context, this use of **will** can express a promise, a threat, or a decision.

   I'll bring you the book tomorrow. (a promise)

   If you do that again, I'll kill you. (a threat)

   We'll go back home at 8.00. (a decision)

Shall

I shall come to London in March.

Some English speakers feel that with the 1st person pronouns (**I** and **we**) **shall** is the correct form, so in formal situations (such as writing business letters) **I will** and **we will** are avoided. It is used to express both a prediction and an intention. However, in normal spoken English there is a contraction to 'll, so the distinction is unimportant. **Shall** in the question form (*Shall I get you an aspirin?*) is different, and is dealt with in Unit 4.

Going to

I'm going to see the doctor this afternoon.
How long are you going to stay in America?

Form

subject + verb + **going** + infinitive to be

Positive

I'm She's They're	**going to** leave soon.

Negative

I'm not You aren't We aren't	**going to** finish.

Question

How long	are you is he are they	**going to stay?**

Use

1 **Going to** expresses a *future intention*, *plan*, or *decision* thought about before the moment of speaking.

   We're going to get married in June.

   When I grow up, I'm going to be a doctor.

Notice the difference between **will** to express an intention and **going to** to express an intention.

A *We've run out of sugar.*
B *I know. I'm going to buy some.*

A *We've run out of sugar.*
B *Have we? I didn't know. I'll buy some when I go shopping.*

The difference is not that **going to** is more certain, and is not about near or distant future, but it concerns *when* the decision was made.

2 **Going to** is used to express a future event for which *there is **some evidence now**.*
Look at those clouds. It's going to rain.
I don't feel well. I think I'm going to faint.
Watch out! Those boxes are going to fall over! Oh dear. Too late.

Notes

1 Notice that **going to go** and **going to come** are often shortened.
When are you going home?
He's coming to see me this afternoon.

2 There are occasions when **going to** to express a future event and **will** for prediction are virtually the same.
This government's policies are going to/will ruin the country.

UNIT 6

Describing People and Places

The Questions

What are the hotels in Rome like?
What does your brother look like?

In Unit 2 we saw **like** used as a *verb*, but in this unit it is presented as a *preposition*. It is important not to confuse them.

Like as a verb is about *pleasures* and *desires*.
Like as a preposition is about *comparisons* and *descriptions*.

Like as a verb

I like coffee, but I don't like tea.
Do you like visiting museums?
What would you like to do tonight?

Like as a preposition

I look like my mother. We both have thick, curly hair and brown eyes. In character, I'm like my father. We're both a bit too critical of other people.
The dress you're wearing is just like one I bought last week.

What's London like?

This means, 'Describe London to me, because I don't know anything about it', or 'What are your impressions of London compared to other cities?' The answer can be a *description* or a *comparison*.

What's London like?
1 *It's quite big, and it's very interesting.* (a description)
2 *It's like New York, but without the tall buildings.* (a comparison)

Be careful not to confuse a description and a comparison.
A *What's Peter like?*
B *He's like tall.* This is WRONG.

What does she look like?

This means, 'Describe her appearance (not her character)'. Again, the answer can be a *description* or a *comparison*.

What does she look like?
1 *She has a plain face, but beautiful, long blond hair.* (a description)
2 *She looks exactly like her sister.* (a comparison)

Again, be careful of confusing the two.
A *What does he look like?*
B *He looks like handsome.* This is WRONG.

How are your parents?

This asks about their health and general happiness only. It does not ask for a description of appearance. Be careful not to confuse it with the two questions above.

A *How's your sister?*
B *She's the same height as me.* This is WRONG.

In some languages *How's your sister?* and *What's your sister like?* are translated by the same question. In English they are different.

How are you?

This is the question we ask friends and acquaintances when we meet them.
A *Hello, Peter. How are you?*
B *OK, thanks. And you?*
A *Fine.*

A *Mr Brown. How nice of you to ring. How are you?*
B *Very well, thank you. And yourself?*
A *Not so bad.*

Comparatives and superlatives

Shakespeare's later plays were more serious than his earlier ones.
What's the longest river in the world?

Form

1 One-syllable adjectives add **-er** and **-est**
cheap/cheaper/cheapest
tall/taller/tallest

In adjectives of *one vowel* and *one consonant*, the consonant is doubled.
big/bigger/biggest
hot/hotter/hottest
thin/thinner/thinnest

2 Adjectives of three or more syllables add **more** and **most**.
beautiful/more beautiful/most beautiful
interesting/more interesting/most interesting

3 Adjectives of two syllables. Those that end in **-er -y -le** are like (1).
clever/cleverer/cleverest
funny/funnier/funniest
simple/simpler/simplest

Those that end in **-ful** or **-ing**, and most other two-syllabled adjectives, are like (2).

careful/more careful/most careful
boring/more boring/most boring
depressed/more depressed/most depressed

Some two-syllabled adjectives take both forms.

polite/politer/politest
polite/more polite/most polite

If you are not sure which one is correct, use **more** and **most**. You will make fewer mistakes!

4 There are some irregular adjectives.

good/better/best
bad/worse/worst

Look at the following examples to see how *comparatives* and *superlatives* are used in sentences.

It's the biggest in the world.
He's the best in the class.
It's the best book I've ever read.

Actions can also be compared.

Riding a bike is easier than riding a horse.
It's nicer to go with someone than to go alone.

5 Constructions with comparisons: *adjectives* and *adverbs*

Positive

As . . . as (*equal comparison*)

She is as tall as me. (adjective)
He speaks French as fluently as a Frenchman. (adverb)

Negative

Not as/so . . . as (*unequal comparison*)

He isn't as/so lucky as me. (adjective)
Your mistake is not as/so bad as his. (adjective)
She doesn't snore as loudly as her husband. (adverb)

Notes

Notice that we also use **as** after **the same**.

Yours is the same as mine.
Frozen peas aren't the same as fresh.

Avoid these common mistakes:
London is as expensive than Paris.

It's the same price than in my country. (WRONG)

UNIT 7
Perfect Tenses (1)

The Present Perfect

I've worked here for ten years.
Have you ever been to America?

Introduction

Foreign students of English often find this tense difficult. The form is similar to a tense in many other Romance languages, but the ideas it expresses are different.
The choice of *Present Perfect* or *Past Simple*, *Present Perfect* or *Present Simple*, is *not about time*.

I've worked as a barman.
I worked as a barman.

Both these sentences refer to the same action in the past. The choice is about *aspect*, that is, how the speaker sees the action. The first sentence is talking about a personal experience in one's life, and the exact time when this happened is not important here. *The Present Perfect relates past to present.*
In the second sentence we expect a time expression to say exactly when in the past this action happened.

I worked as a barman when I was in France.

Form

subject + **have** + past participle

Positive

I've You've We've They've	seen the Queen.

Note **'ve = have**

He's She's It's	worked before.

Note **'s = has**

Question

Where	**have** I **have** you **have** we **have** they	**work**ed before?

Where	**has** he **has** she **has** it	**work**ed before?

Negative

I **haven't** You **haven't** We **haven't** They **haven't**	finished yet.

He **hasn't** She **hasn't** It **hasn't**	finished yet.

Short answers:
A *Have you done your homework?*
B *Yes, I have.*

A *Has she arrived yet?*
B *No, she hasn't.*

Note that we cannot say *Yes, I've* or *Yes, she's.* This is WRONG.

Use

1 **Unfinished past**
The *Present Perfect* is used to express an action or state which *began in the past and still continues*.

I've been a teacher for ten years.
He's had a car since he was 18.

In some languages this is translated by the present tense, but in English this is WRONG.

I am a teacher for ten years is WRONG.

For and since

for	ten years two weeks half an hour ages

for + a period of time

since	August	
	last year	
	Christmas	
	8.00	

since + a point in time

2 Experience

The *Present Perfect* is used to express an action which *happened in the past and is finished*, but we are not interested in *when*. We are interested in the experience as part of someone's life.

Have you ever been in a car crash?

Note that if the time is stated, and if more details are given, the tense changes to the *Past Simple* and the *Past Continuous*.

A *Have you ever had a car accident?*
B *Yes, I have.*
A *When did it happen?*
B *In 1979. I was driving down a road when a car came out in front of me.*

3 Present result

a. The *Present Perfect* refers to a past action and shows the result of that action in the present.

The taxi has arrived.
(It's outside the house now.)

I've recovered from my illness.
(I'm better now.)

She's broken her leg.
(That's why she can't walk.)

b. It is common to introduce news in the *Present Perfect*, because the speaker is emphasizing the event as a present fact.

Have you heard? Mary has had a baby girl.

Again, if more details are given, the tense changes.

Mary had the baby at 6.30 this morning. The baby weighs seven pounds.

Notes

Present Perfect or Past Simple?
a. Compare the different time expressions used.

Past Simple

	yesterday.
	last week.
I did it	two days ago.
	at 8.00.
	when I was young.

Present Perfect

	for a long time.
I've done it	since July.
	before.
	recently.

*Have you **already** done it?*
*Have you done it **yet**?*

b. **Unfinished past**
I've lived in London for six years.
(I still do, and will continue to in the future.)
I lived in Rome for six years.
(At a period in the past, now finished.)

c. **Experience**
I've written two plays.
(Up to now in my life. Perhaps I'll write more.)
Shakespeare wrote about 30.
(He cannot write any more.)

d. **Present result**
Peter has injured his ankle.
(His ankle is still bad.)
Peter injured his ankle.
(We assume the problem is a thing of the past – it happened quite some time ago.)

4 Common mistakes with the *Present Perfect*.

BE CAREFUL. The (a) sentences are WRONG. The correct versions (b) and an explanation are also given.

a. *I have seen him yesterday.* (WRONG)
b. *I saw him yesterday.* (RIGHT)
(Definite time in the past is stated – yesterday – so *Past Simple* is correct.)

a. *I study English for ten years.* (WRONG)
b. *I have studied English for ten years.* (RIGHT)
(Action began in the past and still continues, so English needs the tense that joins past and present – the *Present Perfect*.)

a. *He's been here since two weeks.* (WRONG)
b. *He's been here for two weeks.* (RIGHT)
(The tense is correct, but two weeks is a period of time, so **for** is needed.)

a. *When have you started your job?* (WRONG)
b. *When did you start your job?* (RIGHT)
(The question is asking for a definite time, so the *Past Simple* is needed.)

5 The spelling of the *past participle*.
a. Add **-ed** to the base form of regular verbs.
walked/wanted/picked
b. If the base form ends in **-e**, add **-d**
liked/used/loved
c. A lot of common verbs are irregular. See the list at the end of the Grammar section.

UNIT 8
Expressing Obligation

We have to work to earn money.
He must come and see me as soon as possible.
Do you think I should phone to apologize?

Strong obligation

Form

Must is a modal verb. For an introduction to modal verbs, see pages 90 and 91.

Positive

I You She They	**must** get up early tomorrow.

I You We	**have to** go to work.

He She	**has to** go to work.

Remember the important difference between **must** and **have to**. **Must** expresses the authority of the speaker. **Have to** refers to the authority of another person, or to *obligation* generally. If you are not sure which one to use (to express obligation), **have to** is safer.

Question

Why do	I we you	have to do this?

When does	he she	have to leave?

Must is rare in the question form. When it is used, it is normally in the 1st person (singular or plural).

Must I wear my uniform?
Must we go to this party?

But as a rule, **have to** is preferred.

Negative

You He We	mustn't steal other people's property.

I We	don't have to work if	I we	don't want to.

He She	doesn't have to work on Saturdays.

In the negative they have completely different meanings.

Mustn't = negative obligation/It is not important that you do NOT do something.
Don't have to = no obligation/You needn't, but you can if you want.

Notes

1 **Have to** to express obligation is much more widely used, as it has all the forms of a verb that **must** does not have.

Future: *You'll have to get up early tomorrow.*

Past: *I had to get up at 6.00 to go to school.*

Present Perfect: *I've had to look after my mother for the past ten years.*
Gerund: *I hate having to get up on winter mornings.*

2 **Have got to** also exists in British English to express strong obligation.
Sorry. I've got to tell you the bad news.
Have you got to fly? The train journey is much more fun.

Mild obligation

Form

Should and **ought to** are modal verbs. For an introduction to them, see page 90.

Positive

You He We They	should ought to	learn to relax.

Negative

I You She	shouldn't ought not to (oughtn't to)	work too hard.

Question

Should I Do you think I should	accept the new job?

Use

Should and **ought to** both express *mild obligation*, and so they are often used to give *advice*, and to make *suggestions*.

UNIT 9
The Conditionals

The First Conditional

If you leave before 10.00, you'll catch the train easily.
He won't pass the exam if he doesn't do any work.

Form

Condition	Result
If + present simple,	will + base form of verb

Positive

If it rains, I'll stay at home.

Question

What will you do if you don't find a job?

Negative

If I don't find it, I'll phone you.
If I find it, I won't buy another one.
If I don't work hard, I won't learn.

Use

The first conditional is used to express *a possible condition* and *a probable result*.
According to the situation, it can express different functions.

If you do that again, I'll kill you! (a threat)
Careful! If you touch that, you'll burn yourself. (a warning)
I'll post the letter if you like. (an offer)

Notes

1 Notice that a future tense is not used in the condition.

If you will leave now, you'll catch the train. This is WRONG.

2 Alternative forms:

a. If can be replaced by **unless** or **in case**.

Unless I hear from you, I'll come at 8.00.
I'll take my umbrella in case it rains.
unless = if . . . not
in case = if by any chance

b. Will can be replaced by another modal verb in the result clause.

If you find my money . . .
I can buy you an ice-cream. See Unit 10.
you should give it back to me. See Unit 8.

you must tell me immediately. See Unit 8.

I might buy you a treat. See Unit 12.

c. **Will** can be replaced by an imperative.

If you like good food, eat at Brown's restaurant.

d. **Will** can be replaced by another future tense.

If it doesn't rain, I'm going to play tennis.

This is planned intention. See Unit 5.

e. The *Present Simple* can be replaced by the *Present Perfect* in the conditional clause.

If you've finished this exercise, you can do the next one.

If you've never been to Wales, you should try to go there.

For these uses of the *Present Perfect*, see Unit 7.

The Second Conditional

If I had enough money, I'd eat in restaurants all the time.

If I saw a ghost, I'd run away.

Form

Condition	Result
If + past simple,	would + base form of verb

Positive

If I **won** some money, **I'd travel** around the world.

Question

What **would** you **do** if you **had** £1,000?

Negative

If I **didn't like** my job, I'd give it up.

If I **saw** a ghost, I **wouldn't talk** to it.

If I **didn't work** hard, I **wouldn't have** any money.

Use

The second conditional is used to express *a hypothetical condition* and *its probable result.*

a. The condition is hypothetical because the speaker knows that what he or she is saying is *improbable* or *impossible* or *contrary to known facts.*

I'd lend Peter the money if he needed it.
(Improbable – I know he has enough.)
If I were a bird, I'd fly to you.
(Impossible – I'm not a bird.)

b. The condition can be *possible in theory,* but *improbable in practice.*

If I were the President of my country, I'd abolish taxation.

c. The condition can be an *impossible speculation.*

If we could travel in time, I'd go back to the Roman era.

d. The second conditional can express *advice.*

If I were you, I'd have a rest.
You'd get on with people better if you were more polite.

Notes

1 After **if**, **was** sometimes changes to **were**.
If I were you, I'd . . .
If he were cleverer, he'd . . .

2 Alternative forms
a. **If . . . not** can be replaced by **unless**.

I wouldn't do it unless I loved you.

b. **Would** can be replaced by another modal verb in the result clause.

If I stopped smoking,
I could run faster. See Unit 10.
I might have more money. See Unit 12.

Which conditional?

It is usually clear which conditional to use, but sometimes the difference depends on *how the speaker sees the condition* in a given situation. (This

is called *aspect.* See page 93 for another example of the importance of aspect.)

If I lose my job, I'll . . . (My company is doing badly.)

If I lost my job, I'd . . . (My job is secure.)

If there is a nuclear war, we will . . . (I am pessimistic.)

If there was a nuclear war, we would . . . (I'm sure it won't happen.)

The Zero Conditional

If you heat ice, it melts.

Form

If + Present Simple, Present Simple

Use

The zero conditional expresses *conditions that are always true, with automatic or habitual results.*
If means **when** or **whenever**.
Flowers die if you don't water them.

UNIT 10
Ability and Permission

Can and **could** are modal verbs. (See page 90.) They are used to express *ability* and *permission*.

Ability

She can speak three languages, but she can't write any of them.
I could swim when I was three.
I am writing to inform you that I will be able to attend the interview on June 4. (Formal)

Form

can	
could	+ base form of verb

verb **to be** + **able** + infinitive

	Positive	Negative
Present	can	can't/cannot
	am/are/is able to	am not/aren't/isn't able to
Past	could	couldn't/could not
	was/were able to	wasn't/weren't able to
Future	will be able to	won't be able to

Use

Can, could and be able to all express ability. Can and be able to have the same meaning, but can is more commonly used. Be able to is more formal.

Notes

1 Can has only present and past forms.
Be able to is used for other forms.

  Future: *I'll be able to walk again soon.*

  Present Perfect: *I've never been able to understand your husband.*

  Gerund: *Being able to drive has changed my life completely.*

  Infinitive: *I'd love to be able to help, but I can't. Sorry.*

2 In the past tense, could and was able to are often interchangeable. However, when we are speaking not only of ability in the past but also about successful performance, we must use was able to or managed to.

  The man was drowning, but she *was able/managed to save him.*

3 In the conditional, could and would be able to are interchangeable.

  You could/would be able to run faster if you stopped smoking.

Permission

Could I open the window, please?
You can go home now.
You can't smoke here. It's not allowed.

Asking for permission

Form

Can I	
Could I	*open* the window?

more formal and distant

Do you	
mind if I	*open* the window?
May I	
Would you mind if I opened the window?	

Giving permission

Form

You can	use a dictionary for
You may	the test if you want.

A *Could I sit down here?*
B *Yes, of course.*

A *Do you mind if I sit down here?*
B *No, not at all.*

Refusing permission

Form

You can't smoke in this room.
A *Could I borrow your car tonight?*
B *Actually, I need it myself. Sorry.*

Notes

Be allowed to is also used to express permission.

Are we allowed to use a dictionary?
You're allowed to get married when you're 16 in most countries.
You're not allowed to drive a car without insurance.

Present Perfect Continuous

I've been learning English for three years.
What have you been doing recently?

Form

subject + have + been + present participle

Positive

I've	
You've	
We've	**been** working.
They've	

He's	
She's	**been** working.
It's	

Negative

I	
You	
We	**haven't been** working.
They	

He	
She	**hasn't been** working.
It	

Question

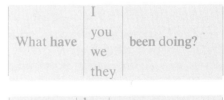

What **have**	I you we they	**been** doing?

What **has**	he she it	**been** doing?

Short answers:
A *Have you been painting?*
B *Yes, I have.*

A *Have you been crying?*
B *No, I haven't.*

Note that we cannot say *Yes, I've*, or *Yes, she's*. This is WRONG.

Use

1 Unfinished past

The *Present Perfect Continuous* is used to express an activity which *began in the past and is still continuing*.

I've been working for the same company for twelve years.
How long have you been playing football?

■ Simple or continuous? ■

There is often little or no difference between such sentences in the simple or the continuous.

I've worked for the same company for twelve years.
How long have you played football?

However, if the continuous is possible, English has a preference for using it.

Certain groups of verbs are rarely found in the continuous. See page 88.

I've known her for 17 years. (NOT *I've been knowing her . . .*
He's had that car for a couple of years. (**Have** = possession)
But *I've been having a shower.* (This is an activity, so it can be expressed in the continuous.)

2 Present result

The *Present Perfect Continuous* refers to a *past activity* and shows the *present result* of that activity.

She's been crying. (Her eyes are red.)
You've been fighting again. (You've got cuts and bruises on your face.)
A *What's that smell* (I can smell it now.)
B *I've been cutting the grass.*

We understand that the activity has recently finished.

Look! It's been snowing. (The ground is all white.)
Look! It's snowing. (*Present Continuous* – it is still snowing.)

■ Simple or continuous? ■

The *Present Perfect Simple* is interested in the *action as a whole*.

A *How are you getting on with your decoration?*
B *I've painted the living room, and now I'm doing the kitchen.*

The *Present Perfect Simple* emphasizes the completed task: 'This is a job that I don't have to think about any more'.

The *Present Perfect Continuous* is interested in the *activity* and in *things that happened as the activity was taking place.*

A *Why have you got paint in your hair?*
B *I've been painting the living room.*

The continuous emphasizes the past activity: 'This is why there's paint in my hair, and this is what I was doing when I spilt some'.

Notes

1 As with all continuous tenses, the *Present Perfect Continuous* expresses *duration* and *activity* over a period of time. Certain verbs by definition do not suggest duration. The action is quickly finished. Examples are:

die/start/begin/finish/stop/find/lose/break.

These verbs are usually found in the *Present Perfect Simple*. Compare these sentences:

a. *I've cut my finger.*
b. *I've been cutting wood.*

Cutting wood can be repeated and can take a long time. When you cut you finger, it is done very quickly. But 'I've been cutting my finger' is a horrible idea, because it suggests that the cutting happened again and again.

2 The *Present Perfect Simple* is interested in the *completed action*. This is why, if the object of the verb has a quantity or number, only the *Simple* is possible.

I've eaten five pieces of toast this morning.
NOT *I've been eating five pieces of toast this morning.*

The five pieces of toast are eaten – the action is completed.

Here are some more examples.

I've been cutting down trees this morning. I've cut down ten.
She's been smoking ever since she arrived. She's had eight already.

3 For the spelling of the present participle, see page 88.

UNIT 12
Future Tenses (2)

The Present Continuous for Future

I'm having lunch with John tomorrow.
We're leaving at 11.00 in the morning.

Form

subject + verb **to be** + present participle

See pages 87 and 88 for examples of the positive, negative, and question forms of the present continuous.

Use

The *Present Continuous* for future expresses a future event that has *already been arranged and planned*.

They're getting married in June. (The church is booked.)
We're leaving at 11.00 in the morning. (Our bags are packed.)

The verbs found in this tense are for the kind of event you would put in your diary, that is, verbs of *activity and motion*.

see *I'm seeing him tomorrow.*
have *We're having a meal together.*
meet *He's meeting me outside the cinema.*
go *We're going on a cruise around the world.*
come *My aunt's coming to stay for a few days.*
leave *She's leaving on the 8th.*
start *I'm starting a new job next week.*

Notes

1 In many languages it is possible to use a present tense to refer to a future event. However, remember

that English has two present tenses. The *Present Continuous* for future is much more common than the *Present Simple* for future.

I'm meeting her at 8.00.
NOT *I meet . . .*

We're going to a party.
NOT *We go . . .*

They're going to Spain next month.
NOT *They go . . .*

They're staying in a hotel.
NOT *They stay . . .*

■ **Present continuous or going to?** ■

The difference between the idea of an *arrangement* for the future (*Present Continuous*) and an *intention* for the future (**going to**) is very small. Once again, the choice depends on aspect (see pages 93 and 96).

a. *I'm going to have dinner with Mary tonight.*
b. *I'm having dinner with Mary tonight.*

a. tells us not only a planned future event, but the speaker's attitude towards it. The dinner is my intention, and so part of my volition. I *want* to.
b. tells us only a planned future event, and nothing of the speaker's attitude towards it. Perhaps he wants to go, perhaps not. It is simply in his diary. Of course, this difference is often unimportant.

2 In the following sentences, the *Present Continuous* is impossible.

It's going to rain tomorrow.
NOT *It's raining tomorrow.*

The sun rises at 5.30 tomorrow.
NOT *The sun's rising at 5.30.*

This is because this sort of event cannot be arranged by human beings.

Might and Could for future possibility.

We might run out of oil before the end of the century.
The weather forecast said it could rain tomorrow.

Form

Might and **could** are modal verbs. See page 90.

subject + **might** + base form of the verb

Positive

I He They	**might** go to America.

Negative

I You We	**might not** see him again.

Question

Do you think	you she they	**might** **will**	come back soon?

Use

Might and **could** express future possibility.

It	**might** **could**	rain, so I'll take my umbrella.

They contrast with **will** to express different degrees of certainty about the future.

She	will		(certain)
	might could	} come tomorrow (possible)	
	won't		(certain)

Notes

1 **Might** and **could** can also express a present possibility.

A *Where's Peter?*
B *He might/could be upstairs. I'm not sure.*

2 **May** can also be used to express a future possibility; usually a greater degree of possibility than **might**.

We may run out of oil.
It may rain tomorrow.
(more likely than *might*)

UNIT 13
The Passive

A lot of foreign cars are imported into Europe.
President Kennedy was killed in Dallas in 1963.

Form

subject + verb **to be** + past participle

All passive tenses are formed in the same way. The tense of the verb **to be** changes to give the different tenses in the passive.

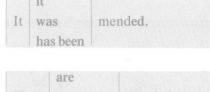

It	it was has been	mended.

They	are were have been	mended.

Present Simple:
Champagne is made in France.
Present Continuous:
The hotel is being redecorated.
Past Simple:
This bridge was built in the eighteenth century.
Past Continuous:
The television was being repaired when it exploded.
Present Perfect:
The building has been knocked down.
Future:
It'll be repaired by next Monday.
This room is going to be painted blue.

The passive infinitive (**be done, be mended, be painted,** etc.) is used with modal verbs.

Experiments on animals should be stopped.
Life might be found on another planet.

Use

Passive sentences move the focus from the *subject* to the *object* of active sentences.

99

John F. Kennedy was shot by Lee Harvey Oswald. (The focus is on Kennedy.)

Notes

1 Very often **by** and the agent are omitted in passive sentences. This might be because:

a. the agent is unknown: *My flat was burgled yesterday.*

b. the agent is unimportant: *The bridge was built in 1876.*

c. it is understood who the agent is: *He was fined £100 for speeding.*

2 The passive is associated with an impersonal style.

Customers are requested to refrain from smoking.
It has been noted that reference books have been removed from the library.

3 The passive can be avoided in informal language.

They're building a new bridge across the Thames.
You don't see many saunas in Britain.

UNIT 14
Reported Speech

There are three areas of reported speech:

1 Reported Statements
He said he would see me tomorrow.

2 Reported Commands
He told them to go back to work.

3 Reported Questions
He asked me where I lived.

Reported Statements

Examples
She said she lived in Rome.
He told me he was going abroad.

Form

He said	he wanted to see you.
Reporting verb	Reported clause

a.

If the reporting verb is in the past tense, it is usual for the verb in the reported clause to move 'one tense back'.

present ▶ past
present perfect ▶ past perfect
past ▶ past perfect

Examples
'I am going.' *He said he was going.*
'She's passed her exam.' *He told me she had passed her exam.*
'My father died when I was six.' *She said her father had died when she was six.* or *She said her father died when she was six.*

b. If the reporting verb is in the *Present Tense*, there is no change of tense in the reported clause.

Examples

'The train will be late.' *He says the train will be late.*
'I come from Spain.' *She says she comes from Spain.*

c. The 'one tense back' rule is not absolute.

Example
'I hate football.' *I told him I hate football.*
(No change to the verb 'hate' – I still hate football.)

d. The 'one tense back' rule also applies to reported thoughts and feelings.

I thought she was married, but she isn't.
I didn't know he was a teacher. I thought he worked in a bank.
I forgot you were coming. Never mind. Come in.
I hoped you would ring me.

e. Some modal verbs change.

can ▶ could
will ▶ would

'Can you type?' *He asked me if I could type.*
'They'll be here tomorrow.' *She said they'd be here tomorrow.*

Others do not change.

would ▶ would
should ▶ should
might ▶ might
could ▶ could
must ▶ must *or* had to

'You should go to bed.' *He told me I should go to bed.*
'It might rain.' *She said she thought it might rain.*

f. There are many reporting verbs.

Say

'Say' is rarely used with an indirect object (that is, the person spoken to).

'Hello everybody,' he said.
She says she's having a lovely time.

Tell

'Tell' is always used with an indirect object in reported speech.

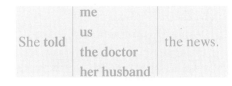

She told	me us the doctor her husband	the news.

Many verbs are more descriptive than *say* and *tell*:

to explain   to interrupt
to admit   to complain   to warn

Sometimes the idea is reported rather than the actual words.
'I'll lend you some money.' *She offered to lend me some money.*
'I won't help you.' *He refused to help me.*

Reported Commands

Examples
He asked me to help him.
They advised us to go home.

Form

Reported Commands nearly all follow the same pattern.

subject	+ reporting verb	+ indirect object	+ infinitive
He	told	them	to go away.
They	urged	the miners	to go back to work.
She	persuaded	her son	to have his hair cut.
I	advised	the Prime Minister	to leave immediately.

Notice the negative command.

*He told me **not** to tell anyone.*
*The police warned people **not** to go out.*

Notes

Notice that 'tell' is used both for reported statements and reported commands, but the form is different.

Reported statement
He told me that he was going.
They told us that he was going abroad.
She told them what had been happening.

Reported command
He told me to keep still.
The policeman told people to move along.
My parents told me not to marry her.

Reported questions

Examples
He asked me what I was doing there.
He wanted to know what time the train left.

Form

a. The 'one tense back' rule is the same with reported questions as with reported statements. (See page 100.)

'Why have you come here?' *I asked him why he had come here.*
'What time is it?' *He wants to know what time it is.*

b. As it is no longer a direct question, the word order is not the word order of a question, and the auxiliary **do** and **did** is not necessary.

'How long have you been here?' *He asked me how long I had been here.* (NOT *He asked me how long had I . . .*)

'Where do you live?' *She asked me where I lived.* (NOT *She asked me where did I live.*)

c. If the direct question is inverted, **if** or **whether** is used.
'Have you been to America?'

He wanted to know	*if* *whether*	*I had been to America.*

Notes

Notice that 'ask' is used for both reported commands and reported questions, but the form is different.

Reported command
I was asked to attend an interview.
He asked me to open my bag.
She asked me not to smoke.

Reported question
He asked me what I did for a living.
I asked him how much the rent was.
I asked him the price.

List of irregular verbs

1 Verbs which are the same in all three forms

Base form	Past Simple	Past Participle
cost	cost	cost
cut	cut	cut
hit	hit	hit
hurt	hurt	hurt
let	let	let
put	put	put
set	set	set
shut	shut	shut

2 Verbs which have the same form for *Past Simple* and *Past Participle*

Base form	Past Simple	Past Participle
bend	bent	bent
bring	brought	brought
build	built	built
burn	burnt	burnt
buy	bought	bought
catch	caught	caught
dig	dug	dug
dream	dreamt	dreamt
feed	fed	fed
feel	felt	felt
find	found	found
get	got	got
have	had	had
hear	heard	heard
hold	held	held
keep	kept	kept
lay	laid	laid
learn	learnt	learnt
leave	left	left
lend	lent	lent
lose	lost	lost
make	made	made
mean	meant	meant
meet	met	met
read	read	read
say	said	said
sell	sold	sold
send	sent	sent
shine	shone	shone
shoot	shot	shot
sit	sat	sat
sleep	slept	slept
slide	slid	slid
smell	smelt	smelt
spend	spent	spent
stand	stood	stood
teach	taught	taught
tell	told	told
think	thought	thought
understand	understood	understood
win	won	won

3 Verbs which have the same form for the base form and the *Past Participle*

Base form	Past Simple	Past Participle
become	became	become
come	came	come
run	ran	run

4 One verb has the same form for the base form and the *Past Simple*

Base form	Past Simple	Past Participle
beat	beat	beaten

5 Verbs which have all forms different

Base form	Past Simple	Past Participle
be	was	been
begin	began	begun
bite	bit	bitten
blow	blew	blown
break	broke	broken
choose	chose	chosen
do	did	done
draw	drew	drawn
drink	drank	drunk
drive	drove	driven
eat	ate	eaten
fall	fell	fallen
fly	flew	flown
forget	forgot	forgotten
freeze	froze	frozen
give	gave	given
go	went	gone
hide	hid	hidden
know	knew	known
lie	lay	lain
ride	rode	ridden
ring	rang	rung
see	saw	seen
shake	shook	shaken
sing	sang	sung
speak	spoke	spoken
steal	stole	stolen
swim	swam	swum
take	took	taken
tear	tore	torn
throw	threw	thrown
wear	wore	worn
write	wrote	written

Tapescript section

UNIT 1

Tapescript 1

Present Continuous: activities in progress

A journalist is interviewing Mr Williams about his job

Journalist What's your job, Mr Williams?

Mr Williams I'm a writer.

Journalist That's interesting. What sort of thing do you write?

Mr Williams Well, uhm, articles for newspapers and magazines, er . . . film reviews, you know, uhm, and occasionally some fiction, poems, and short stories.

Journalist Do you find it a very demanding job?

Mr Williams (sigh) Well, yes and no. It's very nice to work at home, of course, and, and have the choice of when to work. But I work long hours at home, usually ten hours or more a day, and it's very lonely sometimes, sitting in front of a typewriter.

Journalist What are you working on at the moment?

Mr Williams Well, actually I'm doing something very different from my usual work. I'm writing a biography of Leonard Benson, the jazz musician.

Journalist So I suppose you're spending a lot of time together.

Mr Williams (Laugh) Well, no, in fact. He lives in the States. I'm doing a lot of research, naturally. He's visiting this country at the moment, and I have an appointment with him, but we haven't met very often.

Journalist Well, thank you, Mr Williams. That was very interesting and good luck with the book.

Mr Williams Not at all.

Tapescript 2

Present Simple and Continuous

I = **Interviewer**
L = **Mr Leadbetter**

I Mr Leadbetter, I'd like to ask you some questions about your job, if I may.

L Of course.

I Now, you're an engineer, aren't you?

L That's right, I'm a civil engineer. I work for Wimpey, which is one of the largest building contractors in the world.

I That must be very interesting. Could you tell me what you do exactly?

L I work in the estimating department which means I have to work out exactly how much a job will cost. The way it works is like this. Er . . . a company, huh or more probably a country, wants, say, an airport or a bridge or a hospital. They employ a consultant engineer to design it and prepare all the plans. Er . . . then someone has to build it, and this is what Wimpey is, a builder. Well, I then have to say how much I think it will cost to build. I inspect the documents, examine the site where the building is to be, and name a price. If our price is the most attractive, and usually this means the lowest, we get the contract.

I You mentioned airports and bridges. (Mmm, mmm.) What other sorts of construction is Wimpey involved in?

L Oh, what aren't they involved in? (Laugh) Roads, dams, ports, hospitals, universities. Er . . . we do a lot of work abroad, and I often go to the Middle East, which is my specialist area, so I often fly to Saudi and Qatar.

I Er . . . what projects are you involved in at the moment?

L Well, we're building . . . er . . . let me see, we're building a motorway . . . er . . . round London, er . . . the M25, er . . . constructing a railway in Gabon, and we're building a hospital in Oman. Then we're planning several new projects. There's a dam in Swaziland and a university in Jordan.

I Well, thank you very much, Mr Leadbetter. That's most interesting.

Tapescript 3a

Harry's weekend

Harry is American. He works as a sound engineer in a recording studio in San Francisco.

I = **Interviewer**
H = **Harry**

I Harry, could you tell me something about your weekends?

H Sure.

I Are they busy, or . . . don't you do much?

H No, they tend to be very busy. Er, you know I like to . . . er . . . have a good time. I mean, having a good time and enjoying yourself, looking for happiness in life is very important to American people. Uhm so I'm very busy during the week and I . . . I don't have any spare time, so when the weekend comes we like to really let loose and we try very hard to have a good time.

I So what sort of things do you do?

H Well, let's see. It begins on Friday night, of course er . . . we maybe go to a bar for the happy hour, you know, that's when the drinks are half price, er . . . usually we go to the theatre. Er . . . we go to bed early these days. You know, it's not 'in' to go to all-night parties any more, and we want to get up early on Saturday morning anyway. Saturday morning that's the time for cleaning the house, washing the car, doing the laundry, and then it's usually time to go out for lunch. Or maybe brunch, it depends on the time, but it's becoming more popular now to have brunch on Sunday.

I Yes.

H I'll tell you about that in a minute, but . . . after lunch, maybe we'll go for a walk on the beach, or play tennis, or go for a run, you know, er . . . getting physical and getting er . . . fresh air you know somehow, somewhere. Sun . . . Saturday afternoon it's a time to play, really. And then in the evening we sometimes go to a movie, but usually we go to watch a band.

I Oh.

H Yea. Not, not in a concert, in a bar – you know bars in America are more like clubs.

I Oh, yes.

H You know, the music is free, and everything's very relaxed, er . . . and it's nice to just take in some jazz.

I Mmm. So plenty to do on a Saturday.

H Mmm.

I Uhm . . . What about Sunday?

H Well, on Sundays we get an enormous pile of newspapers delivered, and we just . . . er . . . sit in the garden over a cup of coffee, with maybe a continental breakfast and read the newspapers.

I Relax.

H Yea we have a nice quiet morning 'cause er . . . you know you're working up to the most popular meal for the weekend which is brunch.

I That's . . . er . . . breakfast and lunch combined, right?

H That's it. Brunch. It's . . . it's a good time . . . it's a time for all the family, grandparents, and children, and we . . . we usually go out to some restaurant that overlooks the ocean, and you know, you can spend two hours or more over brunch. It's a . . . it's a huge meal. You have all the breakfast things, of course, and then you can also have all sorts of salads, 'n' chicken, 'n' pies, fruit lots of fruit, it just goes on and on and on.

I Uhm . . . Are they expensive these places?

H No, no you pay a fixed price maybe, say, seven dollars per person, and for that you get free champagne and you can eat as much as you like.

I Champagne!

H Yea, it's wonderful.

I O yes, I see, uhm . . . what about Sunday evening then?

H Well, Sunday evening we quiet down a bit. It's time to get ready for Monday. Another week. So we usually have an early night. Maybe watch a little television. We have 88 channels, so you can usually find something you like.

I 88? I'm sure you can. Oh, that's very interesting, Harry, thank you very much.

Tapescript 3b

Svetlana's weekend

Svetlana works in an infants' school during the day, and studies languages at the University of Leningrad in the evening.

I = Interviewer
S = Svetlana

I Svetlana, would you mind telling me about your weekends?

S Well, I often have a lot of university work to do, but if I am free, what I do depends on the time of the year.

I Uhum.

S In winter we often go skiing. My family has a house, a dacha outside Leningrad, and we leave on Friday and come back on Monday morning. Or we play ice hockey or go skating, or go fishing under the ice. All sport is very cheap in Russia.

I Is it? Uhm . . . what about other times of the year?

S Well, you must remember that winter lasts from October to April. In summer we go to the Black Sea, and in autumn something that is very popular is picking mushrooms.

I Really? And where do you do that?

S In the suburbs, in the fields, in the woods around the town, everywhere.

I Ah! Uhm . . . are weekends a special time in any way? Are they for families or time to relax or . . .?

S Well, I don't think they're as special as for you in the west. On Saturday a lot of people work. Children are at school, at least until 1 o'clock and . . .

I Really?

S Yes and usually all day, and most shops are open on Sunday as well. You can do all your shopping on Sunday if you want. Some shops then close on Monday.

I Oh I see.

S People often have a nice meal on Sunday, with all their family, grandparents, grandchildren, and so on. The meal can go on for long time, maybe three, four hours, and we drink vodka and cognac.

I Ah yes. What about entertainment? Do you like going out to the theatre, for example?

S Well, there are lots of cinemas and concerts and ballet, of course. We watch television, mmm but it's not very good. People read lots and lots, popular books and classical as well. We have parties and visit each other a lot. One thing we do is talk to each other on the phone, for hours and hours and hours. If you want to phone someone, it's often impossible because they're engaged all the time. It's very cheap, you see. You just pay a fixed charge, two roubles, 50 kopecs a month.

I Ah! So you don't pay according to how much you use the phone?

S No. That's why we use it all the time.

I That's interesting. Thank you very much, Svetlana.

UNIT 2

Tapescript 4

Jobs: Likes and dislikes

A man is being interviewed about his job.

I = Interviewer
L = Les Mickleby

I Hello, Les.
L Hello.
I It's very kind of you to give me some of your time.
L Ur, that's all right. Now er . . . what do you want me to tell you about?
I Well could you tell me about your job? What do you like about it?
L Well, most of all, I like getting up early in the morning. [laugh] If I live to be 80, I'll say it's because of the fresh air and getting up early, and having a physical job doing physical work. This means a lot to me, because I've always been an active type of person.
I So the early mornings don't bother you?
L No, I've always been an early bird. I used to help the milkman when I was at school.
I What about winter?
L Ar, well, it's a bit harder, but I still like it. Another good thing of course is that I finish early, so I can go to the pub for a pint at lunch-time.
I Ah!
L It's nice to look at other people going to work with their briefcases and things, and think, 'Well, I've done over half my work, I'll be finished at lunch-time.' And some people think it's a boring job. Well, it's certainly repetitive, but you've got to know your area really well to sort the letters.
I Ar yes.
L People are generally very nice, but well, there are some difficult ones. They shout at you for walking on the garden, or for not shutting the gate, or because you

have shut the gate, [laugh] or they park their cars so that you can't actually get to their front door. And of course there's the dogs. One took the top off my finger last year [Oh!] so I don't care for them very much. It's a shame, because I like dogs really, the nice ones, but . . . when there's one going for me I'm terrified of them.
I Ar, I should think so.
L Something interesting is, whether you want to or not, you find out a lot about the people you're delivering to. Perhaps I've never met them, but I know who's having tax problems, who's gone away on holiday, who's having a birthday, and things like that.
I Thank you, Les. You really seem to enjoy your work.
L I do.

Tapescript 5

Children in sport

(BBC Tapescript, You & Yours, Radio 4)

I Hello, and welcome to today's 'You & Yours'. On today's programme we look at children who are trying to be champions in the world of sport, and the pressures they can be under to win, win, win. Now I spoke to Allan Baker, the former British Athletics coach, and he had this to say.
AB Well the problem is that you want to find these children at quite a young age, to train them and motivate them as early as possible. Umm . . . at that age they don't have social problems, you know they don't have boyfriends or girlfriends, so they give their sport the whole of their life. Umm, but they're so young that they can lose their childhood, and they're adults before they're 16. But of course they're not adults at all. Physically they can be quite developed, but emotionally they're still children. Everybody's looking for the new

young star of the future, because there's a lot of money to be earned.
I Tennis is one of the sports where youngsters can play against their elders with more than a chance of success. In America there are tennis schools which accept children from as young as 9. So from the age of 9 a boy or girl is playing tennis for four or five hours every day, and doing ordinary school work around that. I spoke to the team manager of the English Lawn Tennis Association, Pam de Gruchy.
PG You see, we've already seen two 14-year-old American girls, that's Tracy Austin and Andrea Jaeger, playing at Wimbledon, and now, both at 18, they are now already showing the pressures on their bodies and their minds, and people are beginning to question whether this is a good thing for children. A 14-year-old just can't cope with the pressures of Wimbledon, the tournament, the Wimbledon crowds, and the press reporters. Well, I say to my girls, 'Stay at home, stay at school, do the things that teenagers like doing. If you like swimming, well swim; if you like going to dances, just go!' And if when they're older they'd really like to be a professional tennis player, well, they'll be a little older than the Americans, but they'll be better people for it, of that I'm perfectly sure.
I Pam de Gruchy thinks that young players shouldn't be allowed to become professionals until the age of 17 or 18 at least. I asked her what was responsible for the pressures on the young players – was it the money that can be earned, the parents, or perhaps the children themselves?
PG Oh no, it's the parents, without a shadow of a doubt. They want to push their children. I get letters from parents saying, 'My little Johnny enjoys playing tennis all day, and he'd like to learn only that and be trained by a professional coach', and quite frankly I just don't believe it.
I But what about the youngsters

themselves? Robert, a 100-metre and 200-metre runner gave me an idea of his training programme, and his own very simple way of avoiding trouble.

R Well I train under a coach for three days a week, and uhm . . . and . . . then decide how much running to do. If I've trained hard, well then maybe I run five miles, you know, if not so much, then eight miles. Well, of course, I'd like to go to the next Olympics and represent Great Britain, and of course I'd like to win a gold but there are lots of other things I like doing with my life too. Uhm, I, I, play in a rock group and I'm also a keen photographer. Well, I suppose for me the most important thing is enjoyment. If, if you win, you're happy, and if you lose, it's the same. I mean if you start getting upset every time you lose, I think it's time to stop.

I The sports stars of tomorrow, and good luck to them.

UNIT 3

Tapescript 6

Noises for Past Simple and Continuous

Story 1
The wind was blowing.
It was raining.
A dog was barking.
A tree fell down.

Story 2
Someone was driving.
He was listening to the radio.
He was smoking.
He had an accident.

Story 3
The birds were singing.
Bells were ringing.
Someone was snoring.
The alarm went off.

Tapescript 7

A disastrous holiday

I = Interviewer
J = John

I Tell me, have you ever had a holiday that went wrong?

J Oh yes, oh quite a few actually.

I Which was the worst?

J The worst? Well, I suppose it was while I was at university my girlfriend Susan and I had two weeks well no, no, one week, one week of absolute hell and then things got a bit better.

I What happened? Did you fall out, have rows and things?

J No, no it wasn't that. The first thing that went wrong was that the country we were going to decided to have a war a few days before we were going there.

I Oh no!

J Mmm. So that was the end of that. But the plane we were going on was stopping off at Rome. So rather than not having a holiday at all, we thought we'd go to Italy. Very nice. See the sights. Go to the beaches and get fat with pasta. We were at the airport waiting for the plane and a friend of mine who lived near the airport had come to see us off. So we were having a few drinks in the bar and joking with this friend of mine, Peter, saying 'Poor old you in cold rainy England. This time tomorrow we'll be in Italy on the beach.' And I went down to see if the flight had been called and discovered it had gone.

I Oh no! How?

J Well it was a terribly stupid mistake. We hadn't checked the time of departure. I was sure it was going 9 something but it was going at 19 something which of course is 7 o'clock. So we were actually there in the bar when it went without us.

I Oh so what did you do?

J We were determined to have our holiday. The irony was that Peter was not going back to his comfortable home and we were stuck in the cold and the rain at 10 o'clock at night. You see, it was a charter flight so we couldn't book another one. We lost our money and all the other flights were booked up. Well, we got a train to the South Coast and caught the midnight boat across the Channel, froze to death all night, it was a terrible crossing with people being sick everywhere. And eventually we got to I think it was Dieppe and then a train to Paris. We got to Paris very early in the morning and I thought we'd be all right. You see, we now had to hitch hike because a lot of our money had gone on the boat and the train, but I thought 'Well, it's very early in the morning, we'll get a good place to start hitching and we'll soon be well on our way.' We got to the start of the motorway and I just couldn't believe it. I've never seen so many people trying to hitch a lift in all my life.

I Why? What was going on?

J Well, it was then it suddenly dawned on me. It was August the first wasn't it? and on August the first in France the whole population goes on holiday and there were hundreds of people, stopping the traffic, banging on drivers' windows trying to persuade them to stop and give them a lift. It was chaos, disastrous.

I And what happened then?

J Well, we got moving eventually. A lorry driver gave us a lift. And then things started to get better, as we got further south and it got warmer, you know, and we thought 'At last, the holiday's beginning.' Well, we camped that night and we then set off again the next day. We got some lifts, and met a great chap who owned a vineyard. He took us back to his farm and we tasted all this wine – Burgundy, my favourite – and we had a great time. Now the holiday really was starting. Well, he took us back to the motorway, and there we were by the side of the road, the sun was shining, we were a bit merry, sang a few songs – you know, life was great. And we got another lift from . . . well he was a maniac, complete maniac. He seemed nice enough, but within a few minutes he was driving at about a hundred miles an hour, overtaking on the inside on the motorway, with his stereo at full volume, one hand on the wheel and well the other hand on various parts of Susan's body.

I What! So what did you do?

J I don't know why I'm laughing I've never been so frightened in all my life. We were absolutely helpless. Susan tried to say that she had to go to the toilet, but he wouldn't stop then she pretended to be sick in his car, and he stopped in seconds. He had this really flash expensive car, and as soon as he stopped we just jumped out and ran. The worst thing was this tremendous drop from feeling so good to thinking that we were going to get killed.

I Surely that was the end of the disasters, wasn't it?

J Ar yes, just about. We eventually got down to the south of France and began to have a good time, and then down to Italy. We ran out of money, of course, but apart from that, it was good. I've never had such a tiring holiday. When we got back, I was exhausted. At the end of the holiday, I needed a holiday!

UNIT 4

Tapescript 8

Asking people to do things

1

Husband So anyway, I said to him that I didn't think it was right just to give him the job like that without an interview and no job description . . .

Wife Sorry to interrupt, darling. I think the baby's crying. Do you

think you could just go up and see if she's all right? And perhaps give her some milk?

Husband Mmm.

2

Man Yes, madam, can I help you?

Woman Yes, I bought these from here two days ago and the heel's broken. Can you change them?

Man Oh dear. I'm so sorry. I'll just see if we've got another pair for you.

3

Father Turn that wretched music down, will you? Or better still, turn it off.

Child Oh, all right.

4

Woman I think we need an advertising campaign on television and in the press. I really want to push this project. John, would you mind looking after the newspapers, and I'll deal with the television. Is that all right?

Man Mmm, fine. Er . . . when shall we start?

5

Man Anita, will you come here a minute? Could you get me the file on sales in France? I just need to check on delivery arrangements. Oh, and Anita I'd love a cup of coffee if that's at all possible.

Woman Oh yes, Mr James.

6

Man I'm awfully sorry to bother you. I'm sure people are always asking you this as you're always standing here, but you wouldn't have change for a pound, would you? It's for the phone box.

Man Here you are.

Man Thanks a lot.

Tapescript 9

Interview between Anne Catchpole and Mrs. Olive Gibbs
Broadcast 9.11.82, Radio 4
"Woman's Hour" "Released by Arrangement of BBC Enterprises Limited"

A = Announcer
AC = Ann Catchpole
G = Mrs Gibbs

Introduction

A Now at this moment, somewhere on the other side of the Atlantic, Olive Gibbs is probably chugging along the road, in the early morning in her tiny camping van. The travel bug came to Mrs Gibbs rather late in life. About 14 years ago, to help her get over the death of her husband she went on an overland bus trip to Katmandu. This fired her with the enthusiasm to travel more, but as she couldn't afford to go on extensive organized tours, she bought a camper and took to the road alone. Now at the age of 72, she's clocked up about 75,000 miles on trips that have taken her to America, Australia and South Africa. Ann Catchpole met her at her home on the Sussex coast just before she was setting out on her current venture, another wander around America, Canada and Mexico, that'll take about a year, and she'd been very busy that afternoon packing up the van, mainly, as she told Ann, with stocks of food.

Interview

G Of all the meals that I have during the day, my breakfast is the one that I like. It's not that I have a large breakfast but I do like my toast and marmalade. I've got quite a few pounds of marmalade in my van at the moment, I should think I have about 10 pounds, and when that runs out and if I'm down in California by then I shall make some marmalade. I take English things like Marmite which not many other countries of the world seem to appreciate. I'm also taking crisp breads to the United States because I don't care for their bread very much. And I take biscuits because I don't care for their biscuits very much. But otherwise I can buy everything I need in the United States. But I don't like sp . . . wasting my time shopping, so I carry as much as I can and visit a supermarket only when I'm forced to.

AC When you arrive in a country, for example, this trip that you're going on to America, when you arrive, do you have a planned itinerary, or . . . or what?

G Well, I know vaguely which way I'm going to go, but I do change my direction if there's something I hear about which I think I would like to see, or I don't like the road I'll go a completely different way. And at the beginning of the day I don't know quite where I'm going to sleep at night. I wait until I feel tired or I wait until I see somewhere that attracts me and then I stop.

AC What's the reaction when you turn up in your little camper, when you go into these vast American camp sites?

G Well, the first thing I do, and I do this deliberately, I make myself a cup of tea, and I sit outside my van because I think it, it pleases the Americans to see an English lady having afternoon tea. But as soon as I really . . . as soon as I arrive, especially in the United States or Canada, the men all want to talk to me about places they've been to when they were in the army during the war over here. Other people want to know and tell me about where their ancestors came from, and nearly always I have been to the places, or at least know something about them, because I do travel quite a bit in my own country as well as going abroad. In fact when I'm trying to unpack at the end of a day's journey and get a meal in the evening, life becomes very difficult because people gather round and want to know all about me and it's almost dark before I can get on with my unpacking and getting a meal ready. But I do try to get my cup of tea in first.

AC Not only are you a woman, travelling alone, you are now 72. I find that incredible. I mean it's intrepid enough for anybody to set off on a long trip at any age on their own.

G Most people of course are rather surprised, but I'm very healthy. You see, I meet other people who do much more adventurous things than I do. I met a young couple for instance in the United States who were cycling round the United States, and camping. Now I would not camp in a tent. That I should never have a minute's peace. I don't think I should ever sleep but I always think if anybody wants to get at me they're going to have quite a job in a vehicle and you know I can make quite a noise with my horn to attract attention.

AC Have you ever been frightened? Have you ever been in any danger?

G No, not real danger at all. The only time was in Zimbabwe, at that time called Rhodesia, and I was actually camping in Zimbabwe by the Zimbabwe ruins. And during the night someone went by with a torch. It woke me up, and I just thought it was somebody going to a toilet, and I took no notice. But when I woke up in the morning I found that a lot of my papers had been taken, and the wallet in which I kept them. And of course I didn't realize at the time what was going on. It must have been the noise of the door closing which woke me up. I suppose I'm very foolish but often I don't lock myself in my van at night. Sometimes I do if I feel at all nervous or if I'm in a camp site on my own, then I do lock myself in.

AC Where would you say in all your thousands of miles of travel on your own you've been happiest?

G In a way it's difficult to say because each country has something special about it. But I think the beauty of South Africa is something that I shall never forget. I used to stand sometimes when I was there and say to myself, 'Just look and look as much as you can in case you don't come this way again.'

UNIT 5

Tapescript 11

The weather

And now here's the weather forecast for the next twenty-four hours for the whole of England, Wales, Scotland, and Northern Ireland. Ah starting with Southern England and the Midlands, well it'll be mainly dry and sunny, but quite cold, with temperatures around six or seven degrees celsius. It should stay dry all day, but there'll be quite a wind, so wrap up warm.

And the west country, Wales and Northern Ireland. You can expect some rain in the morning and afternoon and quite strong north easterly winds, and the temperature will be lower than yesterday, around the three or four degrees mark. I don't think you'll see much of the sun: cloudy all day, I'm afraid. The East coast of England will see the best of today's weather. It'll be warmer than yesterday, no winds, and sunshine, so quite warm for the time of year.

In Scotland and Northern Ireland, however, there'll be heavy rain and maybe some snow during the afternoon, and on the hills temperatures will drop to below freezing, minus four or five, and on the highest spots minus ten. Over much of Scotland it will be cloudy, and windy too as the cold front moves in over the Atlantic. Northern Ireland can expect the same, but the rain will end before dark. But again very cold, with temperatures not going above freezing.

And that's all from me.

Tapescript 12

Phone-in on China

P = Presenter   T = Miss Townsend
A = Mr Atkins   C = Mr Cannings
L = Kate Leigh
J = Mrs Jackson
S = Dr Scott

P Hello and good morning.
On today's programme we turn our thoughts to life in the People's Republic of China, that vast country of over one thousand million people. One out of every five people in the whole world is Chinese. It's the third largest country, smaller only than the Soviet Union and Canada. It has a recorded history of nearly four thousand years, and, would you believe, it has the only man-made object visible from outer space, the Great Wall.
But what is life like for the ordinary Chinese citizen? What sort of housing, education, medical treatment do they have? They've recently opened their doors to the rest of the world. What can we now learn about them?
With me are two people who can answer many of these questions. They are Dr Henry Scott, from a London University, and Kate Leigh, who spent several years teaching English at the University of Peking. Now known as Beijing. Our number is, as usual, 01 423 1838. And our first caller is Mr Atkins. What is your question please?

A I'm going to spend a year in China soon, studying Chinese language and history at university, and I wondered if you could give me some idea of what life might be like, what sort of reception to expect, and what sort of life style I'll have?

P Kate . . . er . . . this sounds like a question for you.

L Good morning Mr Atkins.

A Good morning.

L Er . . . let me ask you a question first. Which university are you going to?

A To the university of Jinan, in the north.

L Oh, yes, that's the capital of the province of Shandong. Well, you'll live in the university, nearly all foreign visitors do, and you'll share a room with a Chinese student, which is also very common. Days start very early, so

you'll have to get used to getting up at about six o'clock. There are morning exercises in the open air, and you'll be invited to join in, and then you'll have breakfast at about six thirty. And all meals are communal. Now your classes will probably be in both English and Chinese, and they'll begin at seven thirty. Lunch is at twelve and then there's a rest until three, and then more classes until six.

A Er yes, yes and could I ask, what sort of things people do in the evening?

L Well, the main entertainments are going to the cinema, which everybody does at least twice a week; in fact it's difficult to get tickets; going for walks; sitting outside talking, playing cards; there are always lots of people in the streets, uhm there are few cars but literally millions of bicycles; and eating out, and of course Chinese food is legendary.

A Er yes, well, thank you very much.

P And now let's go on to our second caller, Miss Townsend. Hello.

T Hello.

P What is your question please?

T Er yes. I'd like to ask in what way China is different now from a few years ago? Their policy seems to have changed. I wondered how and why?

P Thank you. Uhm Dr Scott, can you help us with this one?

S Mmm. Yes. Good morning Miss Townsend.

T Good morning.

S Now this is a very big question, of course. China has been a Socialist Republic since 1949 under the leadership of Mao Tse Tung. He started the Cultural Revolution in 1966, and that continued until his death in 1976. China is now in the hands of Deng Xiaping, who has given the country a little free enterprise. Doors are now open to the rest of the world. China wants the technology and the education that the rest of the world can offer; it is anxious to trade, and it is offering many interesting contracts. The

industry it most wants to develop is tourism. China is trying to build a better life for its people without turning its back on its ancient culture that gives its people such pride and dignity. So . . . uhm . . . yes, times are changing.

T Thank you that's most interesting. Thank you very much.

S Pleasure.

P And on the subject of tourism, we now have another caller, Mrs Jackson, who I believe is going there on holiday. Mrs Jackson, hello.

J Yes, good morning. I'm going on a tour of China with a holiday company, and I noticed that all arrangements in China are handled by China International Travel Service. Could you tell me if I'll be able to travel freely in China, and how much contact I'll have with the Chinese people?

P Kate, please could you give us your thoughts on these questions?

L Yes, certainly. You will probably spend most of your holiday with the tour company, who'll decide with the Travel Service where you'll go. There are in fact many cities that you can visit with just the ordinary visa, and others that you need to get a visa from the local police station to go to. Now there is a very good train service and also an internal air service, but I recommend the trains as you'll see so much more of the country. However, how much you'll see of the people is a different matter. Foreigners are not allowed to have the local currency. They are issued with their own money which can only be used at certain places, so well I'm afraid, you won't be able to buy things in the street for example. Now you must remember that almost no-one speaks English, so I strongly recommend you learn some Chinese before you go. It's a very different way of life. The Chinese are friendly, honest, terribly proud of their country and the progress it's made, enthusiastic,

109

and they'll be very interested in you, where you're from, what you do, how you live, everything. You must remember that tourism is still in its infancy. If you go with the right attitude, your visit to China will be one of discovery, and well . . . it'll be a very memorable experience.

J Thank you very much.

P And now we have a question from a Mr Cannings. Hello, Mr Cannings.

C Hello, yes, er yes, yes. I'd like to ask about the food. Are the Chinese restaurants we have here typical of the food you find there?

P Thank you. Dr Scott.

S Good morning Mr Cannings. Well, Chinese cuisine is rightly famous in the whole world. I mean, sweet and sour sauce, beef and green peppers, garlic . . .

UNIT 6

Tapescript 14

Match the answers and questions

1 She's very nice, actually. You'd really like her. She's the kind of person you can always go to with a problem.

2 She's not too good. Still got a temperature and a cough that she can't shake off.

3 Her greatest passion is horse-riding. She lives for horses from morning till night.

4 I can't stand her. She's everything I don't like in a woman. She's bossy, she's superior, and she thinks she can do everything better than other people.

5 Very plain. Long straight hair, high forehead, and prominent cheek bones.

6 She's fine. Very happy since she met Bernard, and she seems to be very well, too.

7 Mmm . . . A bit like you, actually. Same build, same height, and similar colour eyes.

8 She's quite good-looking. The kind of girl you go for. But she's a bit too serious for me. You know, politics, literature, human rights, things like that.

9 Gardening, cooking, and sailing, in that order.

10 The doctors say she'll be in hospital for at least another week.

Tapescript 15

Who are these people describing?

1 She's absolutely adorable. I think she's very pretty, she makes me laugh a lot, um . . . she tells terrible jokes but I like the way she tells them. She's a bit naughty sometimes and I curse her when she gets me up at six o'clock in the morning, but when I hear her singing in the morning, well, all is forgiven. She can twist me round her little finger, of course.

2 He was very boring and predictable. The kind of person who remembered birthdays and anniversaries, but who made you angry because there was absolutely nothing spontaneous about him. His ideas of fun were so unadventurous. Well, the first few years were OK, but after that I'd just had enough. Reliable, stable, dependable, and boring.

3 Well, he's quite well-dressed and punctual. Sometimes he's cheerful and tells us jokes, but other times we have to do a lot of work. We don't really know him very well. Oh, I know he's married, but I've never met him socially or anything like that. He seems very professional.

4 I've never actually spoken to him. Mmm, I see him every day, of course, as he leaves his car and gets in the lift to his office on the top floor. He's always terribly well-dressed, and he must wear expensive after-shave because you can still smell it ten minutes after he's gone.

Tapescript 17a

America as seen by Britons

Bob and Sheila spent two years living in New York because of Bob's work as a banker. Neither of them had lived in a big city before. They now live back in England in a small village outside London.

I = Interviewer
S = Sheila
B = Bob

I How long did you live in the States?

B We were there for two and half years, in New York.

I And did you enjoy it?

S Oh, tremendously. We had a wonderful time.

B Yes, what I liked best was that I could work and still lead a normal life. I mean, the shops are open till 10 o'clock.

I All shops?

S Yes, everything, food shops, chemists . . .

B There's a huge department store called Gimbles on 86th Street that was open till 9.00.

S And some supermarkets are open twenty-four hours a day. Most shops don't open as early as in England, well they don't open until about uhm . . . 10 or 11 in the morning.

B Yes, that's right.

S Because they all work much later. And everything's open on Sundays.

B And the holidays, the public holidays are much shorter than here, and in the States only the banks are shut. Everything else stays open, so it makes life much easier. You could do what you liked when you liked.

S And it was easier with the children, because I could wait till you got back and we did the shopping together, didn't we?

B Yes.

I I see, um . . . do you think New York is as cosmopolitan as London?

S Oh yes, but it's not as mixed. Nationalities stay in their own areas; like there's the Ukrainian section, the Russian section . . .

B . . . the German section. We were in German Town, York Town, which is called German Town. And there was a row of German shops, all German-speaking.

S Yes.

B But you didn't find that anywhere else. And the Ukrainians were down on 14th and 2nd, and the Spanish kept to Spanish Harlem.

S I think the major difference was the height of the place. Everything was up. We lived on the twenty-ninth floor.

B And I worked on the sixty-third floor.

S But I like heights. And of course everything is faster. And the people are much ruder.

B Which means of course that we're much ruder ourselves now we're back in Britain.

I Oh, in what ways?

B Well, pushing in the street.

S Oh, I don't!

B Fights about getting on the bus. No good old British queues.

I But, are all Americans like that?

S Oh yes. Well, all New Yorkers anyway. Not so much in other places. When we went to California it was very different. There weren't the same pressures at all, were there?

B I think we were aware that New York is quite a dangerous place. We never had any problems at all, but when there was a crime, it was horrendous.

S Oh yes, the subways are unusable. They're dirty, uncomfortable.

I Did you make many friends?

S Well, that's what's interesting really. We made more friends there than we have after two years of living here. I think Americans are more open, they, you know, they speak their minds, so if they don't like something, they actually tell you directly. Not like the British, who might think one thing and say another. So I suppose you could say that the English are ruder than the Americans.

B Or that they're less honest.

S Mmm. Yes.

B Something else. We're actually moving from here back into London to try to find the things we liked in New York, but I don't suppose we'll find them.

Tapescript 17b

England as seen by Americans

Terry Tomsha talks about her experience of living and working in England, where she has been for the past eleven years.

I = Interviewer
T = Terry

I So, Terry. You've been in this country for quite a long time now.

T Mmm.

I What differences do you notice between the two countries?

T Obviously the biggest difference is the people. The average Englishman is . . . mm cold and not very open.

I Oh.

T In the States it's very different. We start conversations with people in the street, in the subway; we're a lot more enthusiastic and spontaneous than people here. You know, when I first came, I couldn't understand why I was getting so little reaction from people, but now I see that they thought I was overpowering and that I was trying to be too friendly too soon.

I But, tell me; does the Englishman improve as you get to know him?

T Oh yes.

I Oh good.

T Once you have made a friend, it's a friend for life, but it takes a very long time. I'll tell you something that I think is very important. An Englishman in America is respected. Everyone wants to talk to him. We're inquisitive, we love his accent and his country. An American though in England is thought to be a little inferior because of his behaviour and his language. One thing I've learned – it's funny now, but it wasn't at the time – I couldn't understand why when I was talking to someone he would move away, you know, move backwards, and I thought 'Do I smell? Am I boring him?' The reason was, you see, Americans stand closer when they're talking. Again, English people like a certain distance.

I That's true. What about your impressions of living here? How does that compare with the States?

T Well, mmm . . . I think life's a lot easier in the States. It's easier to make money and it's easier to spend it. Shops are open all the time over there. Here you've got to race to reach the supermarket by 5.30. Generally though I find life more inefficient here. If you need an electrician, it takes days to get one, he doesn't do the job very well, the system is so old that he can't get the parts to repair it, and he doesn't care.
This leads to another very important point. Americans work a lot harder than you do. To the English their private lives are important, their holidays are important, their gardens are important, their animals are important, but an American wouldn't admit that. For us, our work is the most important thing in our lives. You know, holidays seem to be longer here, people make the most ridiculous excuses not to go to work – 'My dog's got a cold', I heard the other day.

I Oh, come on.

T You have tea breaks that get longer and longer. In that respect we're quite like the Japanese. Our jobs come first, but there are all sorts of services to make life easier around our jobs.

I Well, I take it you have a pretty negative opinion of England.

T You would think so from this interview, wouldn't you? No, in fact I really love it here. I go home once a year and really look forward to coming back here. This is my home now. I find life safer, more relaxed, and much more enjoyable. Maybe I've gotten into English habits! England doesn't have the dramatic beauty of the States, but oh, it is very pretty and charming in a way that I find comforting.

UNIT 7

Tapescript 20

A retired man

I spoke to Mr Harold Thomas about the pleasures and problems of retiring after over thirty years in the business world. He used to be managing director of a textile company employing over 300 people, and I asked him how his life has changed since he'd retired.

I = Interviewer
HT = Harold Thomas

HT Well, I've been retired now for nearly five years, so I've had plenty of time to adapt to it. Well, obviously my life has changed a lot. Now I have time to do all the things I've always wanted to do, and I'm lucky that I still have the health to do them.

I Could you give me some examples of the kind of things you've done?

HT Yes, well I've taken up golf, which is just the right sport for an old man. Well, it's not really a sport at all, at least, not the way I play it. It's a good excuse to go for a walk, and from time to time you have to hit a ball into some water. What I like is that I've made some good friends at the golf club, and I see quite a lot of them. There's one couple in particular that I've met, same age as me, and we've got very friendly. We've even been on holiday together a few times. We went to Wales last summer.

I Do you go away more now? I mean I can see you're very brown.

HT Yes, I've just come back from visiting my son in Malaya. Oh yes, I've been to all sorts of places. Portugal, Morocco, Turkey, and I went on a cruise to Egypt at Easter. That was lovely. Well, you have to fill the time somehow.

I Do you find that a problem, filling time?

HT Uhm yes, yes I think so. You see, I lost my wife two years ago, and after 35 years of being together, you really miss . . . well, I, I, really miss her. So uhm, I have to keep myself busy. I've started doing some community work, just driving people around who aren't mobile on their own, to help with shopping and visiting people and going to hospital appointments and things like that, you know. As you get older you begin to realize the things that are important to you. Of course you begin to regret things, too, but I mean that's inevitable. Something I've done recently is get in touch with all the relatives I haven't seen for years. You see I went to a funeral two months ago in the village where I was born, and I passed the house of a girlfriend I hadn't seen for thirty years. So I called in and do you know, she remembered me after all this time. We started talking about my family and she knew where some of my cousins had moved to, so I traced them and that started it all. Now I'm trying to find the others all over the country.

I Do you enjoy retirement?

HT Some of the time yes, and some of the time, no. I think I've deserved this rest after a full working life, but I do wonder sometimes what the point of it all is. You know . . . I miss the direction and discipline that work gives you. So I just take each day as it comes.

UNIT 8

Tapescript 21

Phoning a landlord

Angela is a student at university. She is looking for a room to rent. She saw an advertisement and has decided to phone the landlord.

A = Angela
L = Landlord

L Hello. 678 5423.

A Hello. I saw your advertisement for the room.

L Oh, oh yea. That's right.

A I wonder if you could give me some more information?

L Yea, well, well what would you like to know?

A Well, I was wondering . . . Er . . . What's the rent?

L £35 a week.

A And what does that include?

L The room, obviously. It's your own room. You don't have to share. It's a single room. You share the bathroom and you can use the kitchen, but there's no meals included.

A Right, uhm . . . and what about heating?

L No, no you don't have to pay for that. There's central heating in all the rooms, so there's nothing extra to pay there.

A Oh lovely, and do you want the rent weekly? Is there a deposit?

L You have to pay weekly, on a Monday. And there's a one-week deposit, payable in advance.

A Right, that sounds fair. Are there any particular house rules, you know, that I've got to keep to?

L How do you mean?

A Well, like what about guests and hours?

L Oh yea, well you can come and go as you want, of course, but you must pay a deposit for the front-door key. That's separate from the other deposit, I'm afraid.

A I see

L As for guests, they should be out by eleven o'clock. We don't like to say that, but we've had a bit too much trouble, so we have to say it.

A Right. Is it quite near public transport?

L Oh yes. Five minutes to the tube station, and the bus stop is just round the corner with buses into town every ten minutes or so.

A Lovely, it sounds very interesting. Do you think I could come and have a look at it this evening?

L Yea, of course. I'll give you the address. Now, it's 35, Chestnut Avenue, Walton. How'll you be coming?

A By car.

L Well, it's just by the police station and the library.

A Yes, well I know it. If I come about eight is that all right?

L That's fine. Could you tell me your name?

A Angela Smiley.

L Right. I'll see you around eight. Goodbye.

A Bye-bye.

Tapescript 22

First aid

I = Interviewer
C = Dr Clarke

I Dr Clarke, when an accident happens the people present are much more likely to be people of the general public and not members of the medical profession. Now, how good are we? I mean would you say that a little knowledge is a dangerous thing? If we're not sure what to do, is it actually best not to do anything at all?

C Well, they're obviously interesting and important questions. Yes, first aid is terribly important and you can save lives if the right action is taken. I'd say that uhm ninety per cent of first aid is common sense, and only ten per cent is specialist knowledge. If someone isn't breathing, you must give them artificial respiration, and I think most people know how to do that. If

the person is bleeding, the bleeding must be stopped. I think these things are obvious. Medical help must of course be sought and someone must decide whether the victim can be taken to hospital, or whether, given the nature of their particular accident, the victim should be left alone.

I Yes, can we talk about road accidents more specifically in a moment?

C Yes.

I Is there one particular kind of accident where generally we get it wrong, we follow our common sense but it lets us down, and we do the wrong thing?

C Yes, I think there are two things associated with that. On the subject of burns, for example, some people put cream or grease or butter on, and this in fact makes the burn hotter; and the other thing . . .

I I'm sorry to interrupt. What should we do about burns, then?

C Well, you need to decide first of all how bad it is. If it is a minor burn, the best thing to do is put the burnt area under the cold tap, or slowly pour on iced water.

I I see.

C This should be done for about ten minutes, and it stops the heat from spreading. However, if it's a bad burn, what we call a third-degree burn, don't touch it, you really should get for this kind of burn expert help immediately. Cover the burn very lightly with something clean like a sheet or a, or a handkerchief and then go straight to a hospital. The other thing people do is to give drinks, especially alcoholic drinks, which means that if the patient needs an operation, we can't give an anaesthetic.

I So it's better not to give any drinks at all.

C Certainly not alcoholic drinks. If the patient complains of thirst, he should wash his mouth with water and not swallow.

I That's very useful. Now back to road accidents. Could you give us some general advice on what to

do at the scene of a car accident?

C Yes. Three things. First of all you should check that the victims are breathing. I mean if they're not, give artificial respiration. The most common injuries in car accidents in fact are fractures and bleeding, so the second thing to do is stop the bleeding. Thirdly, er . . . very important don't move the victim unless it's absolutely necessary. I mean, if any bones are broken, the injury could be made much worse by moving the victim. You should keep them warm, loosen any tight clothing, and try to reassure them. They'll probably be suffering from shock, so just stay with them until expert help arrives. It's a very good thing to do.

I Right, I see. Now, of course, there are a lot of accidents we haven't had time to talk about. But do you think it's worth while for the general public to find out about them, and find out how they can help?

C Sure, sure, yes, yes. I do indeed. I mean, I would advise people to find out as much as they possibly can. I mean, many of us freeze and panic when faced with a crisis. So, you know, why not learn about basic first aid?

I Dr Clarke, thank you very much.

UNIT 9

Tapescript 24

A house to buy

L = Linda
J = Jeremy

J What did you think of that place, then? Not bad, was it?

L Oh, it was lovely, it was really lovely. A very pretty house, a beautifully modernized cottage.

J Mmm. Not as big as the house we've got at the moment, though.

L No, not as big, it's true, but it's in a much better location, with the countryside all around, and lovely views from the bedrooms.

J It's quite a long way from the station, isn't it? If we bought it, we'd have to drive to the station, we couldn't walk.

L That wouldn't matter. You can walk in summer if it's a nice day. It's a lovely walk across the park.

J I'll tell you one thing I didn't like, actually, and that was the low ceilings everywhere, especially in the kitchen.

L Yes, but think how expensive it is to heat our house at the moment, and that's partly because the ceilings are so high. If the ceilings were lower it would be much cheaper to heat. I mean our gas bills would really go down.

J I suppose you're right. But the lounge is tiny. You couldn't get more than five people in it.

L Yes, I know, but the thing to do with this house is to knock down the wall between the living-room and the dining-room. Then you'd have a good-sized room. And think how cosy it would be on a winter evening, beside that open fire. And the kitchen was big, anyway. And nice and bright.

J Mmmn . . . I'm afraid I didn't like the bedrooms very much, with one on the first floor and another two in that converted loft.

L Oh I loved the bedrooms, particul. . . well, *all* the bedrooms. They're all double bedrooms, and with those views . . .

J But the main one, the main one is right next to the street, so that would be very noisy.

L But the street isn't so noisy. I mean, it's only a lane, it's not really a busy road. You wouldn't hear very much.

J Yes, true. And I suppose the children can have the bedrooms on the top floor. The stairs are a bit dangerous. I'd have to fix them. And the roof is leaking. If they don't do something about that soon, the ceiling will come down. It's been raining a lot recently.

L What about the outside? What did you think of that?

J I thought it was very attractive,

with the courtyard and then the garden. I bet the courtyard catches the sun. We could eat out in summer.

L And it's quite a big garden. And that's a lovely mature apple tree right in the middle. Lots of space for your vegetables. So what do you think?

J Well, I'm not so sure. I don't think it would be big enough for us.

L OK. Think again, then.

UNIT 10

Tapescript 25

The nine o'clock news

Here is the nine o'clock news.

Last night thieves stole a painting from the home of Lord Bonniford. The painting, a sixteenth-century masterpiece by Holbein, is said to be priceless.
Lord Bonniford said he could hear noises in the middle of the night, but he paid no attention. The security guard, Mr Charles Potts, couldn't phone the police because he was tied hand and foot.
The thieves managed to get in and escape without setting off the security alarm by cutting off the electricity supply.

Andrew Gardener, the man who had a liver, heart and kidney transplant, is doing well after his operations, say his doctors.
Andrew is able to sit up and feed himself. He can get out of bed but he can't walk yet, as he is still too weak. Doctors say he'll be able to go home in a few weeks' time.

Tapescript 28

Permission or request?

Listen to these dialogues. A man called Dick is talking to five different people.

1 D = Dick   O = Operator

D Hello.
O Hello.
D Hello. Could you tell me the code for Rome, Italy please?
O Are you dialling direct?
D Yes.
O One moment. It's 010 396, followed by the number.
D Thank you, Goodbye.

2 D = Dick   M = Megan

D Megan!
M Mmm?
D Could you do something for me? Can you see the paper over there? Could you get it for me?
M Sorry, where is it?
D On the television.
M OK.

3 C = Charles   D = Dick

C There you are, sir. That'll be £35.50.
D Can I pay by cheque?
C Cheque, credit card, cash, any way you like.
D Who do I make the cheque payable to?
C British Rail, please, sir.
D And do you need my cheque card?
C Oh yes, please.
D There you are.
C Thank you. And here's your ticket.

4 B = Bernadette   D = Dick

B Hello.
D Hello. I wonder if you could help me? Would you mind if I left my bags here just for one minute? I have to make a phone call.
B No I'm sorry, sir. It's not allowed.
D It's only for a short time.
B It's against regulations. No baggage can be left in reception for security reasons.
D Is there anywhere I can leave them?
B I'll get a porter to take them to the left luggage office.
D Where's that?
B It's next to the dining room.

D No, don't bother, it doesn't matter.

B Pardon?

D I said don't worry. It's OK.

5 **D** = Dick **A** = Anna

D Excuse me?

A Yes.

D Would you mind if I went before you? I have to make a very quick call, but it's really urgent.

A Er . . . er . . . No, go on, that's fine.

D Oh, that's very kind. Thank you.

Tapescript 29

Educating children at home

Broadcast 9.4.84, Radio 4,
"Woman's Hour"
"Released by Arrangement with
BBC Enterprises Limited"

I = Interviewer
B = Bruce Cox

I Now educating children at home is something that apparently twice the number of parents are taking on than used to be the case. It's been estimated that about 6,000 children are being taught at home without going to school. 'Education Otherwise' is the name of one organization of parents who've taken this step, and Bruce Cox is one of their members. He's joined me in our studio with June Fisher, who's Head Teacher of Catford County School, that's a girls' comprehensive in south London, and I know June is familiar with what's called 'de-schooling' children from a teacher's point of view. Bruce, first of all, it's not against the law, is it, to take your children out of school or not to put them in school?

B No, it's . . . it's um . . . Children must be educated, according to the 1944 Act, but whether you educate them in school or otherwise, is a matter for parents to choose.

I Now, how have you done that with your children, and why have you not sent them to school?

B Well, we have three children, none of them went . . . have been to school until very recently, when they started at . . . um . . . to go to a small . . . um . . . school that's run by a co-operative group of parents.

I That is an alternative school?

B An alternative school, yes, a part-time school really. We didn't send them to school in the first place for a variety of reasons. It wasn't a sudden, big, dramatic decision. And we realized that Eleanor would have to be bussed off to a remote . . . um . . . school, that we would say goodbye to her at eight o'clock and see her again . . . at . . . sometime after half past four. Um . . . we didn't like that. We . . . we'd been involved in play-groups, and had a pretty clear idea of what went on in infant schools and felt . . . well, we weren't particularly hostile to school in some respects, um . . . that we could do just as good a job. And we very much enjoyed having our family all together at home.

I Now your boy is 6 and your girls are 9 and 11. Do they have a curriculum at home?

B We don't have a curriculum in the sense of . . . um . . . er . . . an organized programme of work that we solidly go through. Um . . . we've done a certain amount of more organized maths, but most of the things we do arise out of the ordinary business of day-to-day life and responding to their interests and questions.

I Can you give an example of that?

B Well, it may be that er . . . they may be interested in growing something in the garden, so they may have a plot of land that they can grow things in, and . . . see them come up. It may be that they're interested in drama, so they go along and join a drama club, and eventually they are involved in some kind of production. It may be that er Eleanor and Madeleine are, that they're very interested in gymnastics, so again they go along to a club and enjoy that.

I That all sounds rather lovely. I mean, I would have loved to have been educated like that. But what about the three Rs, reading, writing and arithmetic? I mean, how good are they at doing those things, and are you confident that they're keeping up with their school peers?

B Well they're perfectly um . . . they're perfectly OK as far as reading and writing are concerned, though we've been much more happy to leave the direct teaching of it to a later point in their lives than perhaps would happen at school. But I think that has worked out very well.

I So you're suggesting that perhaps they're not quite up to their peers in terms of writing.

B Oh no, I think, I think that they are, but I think that we have left it until a bit later er . . . to introduce direct teaching to them.

I You're a qualified teacher, Bruce. Who does all the teaching at home?

B Well, this has largely been the responsibility of my wife, who isn't a qualified teacher, and I would . . . sort of hasten to add you don't have to be a qualified teacher to educate your children at home. Most people who do educate their children at home aren't qualified in any way.

I When you were at school, what were your own feelings about school? I wonder if what your children are undertaking now stems from some sort of feeling about school that you had?

B No, I don't think it stems from anything that I experienced at school in itself. I think it stems partly from my experience as a teacher. At school I was quite successful, I quite enjoyed it. I did think that it was very dependent on the 'carrot and stick' motivation.

I   But could you get expert help if you felt that you weren't capable of taking a child up to maths or English O or A level? Can you go outside educating your child at home for expert help? This costs money sometimes, presumably.

B   Erm . . . Well, certainly if you're doing correspondence courses it costs money. I don't think the cost is exorbitant, but it does cost money. I think that we could easily underestimate the immense reserves of expertise and good will that exist in a community once you start trying to dig it out. The range of people that have helped us, or been prepared to help us or have helped other families. People are delighted that somebody comes along and asks them for knowledge to be shared that they have.

UNIT 11

Tapescript 32

Charity appeals

1   This might be the age of high technology in many western countries, but for the majority of the world's children, everyday life is still a fight just to survive. In Africa and Asia, ten per cent of babies die before they are one year old. Average life expectancy is about 46. One in four Third World children can expect to suffer malnutrition. In developing countries nearly three quarters of the people do not have access to safe water, yet eighty per cent of the world's disease is caused by dirty water.
Action Aid has started development programmes in eight of the poorest countries in the world. Our sponsorship scheme is based on the belief that individual people relate much more easily to the needs and problems of one other person than to the statistics

expressed in millions. Sponsorship is a personal relationship with one child in need, and sponsors have a link with the child, either through reports on progress at school or by direct correspondence. Our first aim is to provide a basic education and, where needed, food, clothing, and medical care.
Over the years we have helped more than half a million children, but we need your help to continue. You can give a child a chance. Just contact a branch of Action Aid.

2   Mencap is the Royal Society for Mentally Handicapped Children and Adults. It has been operating since 1946, and has grown into an organization with 55,000 members, most of whom are parents and friends of mentally handicapped people. Mental handicap is not an illness; it cannot be cured by medical means, it is a life-long disability. Our aims are to educate the general public and to provide the care that the mentally handicapped need. About one in every hundred people is affected by some form of mental handicap. Most of the rest of us know very little about it. But our ignorance and fear can mean that we treat these people in a way which is hurtful and discouraging to them.
We have opened two new residential homes for children this year, and we have been trying for several years to find residential accommodation for mentally handicapped adults whose relatives are no longer capable of looking after them. It is for this, and our many other projects, that we need your help. Please give generously.

3   Amnesty International will only be satisfied when it is no longer needed. We are a worldwide movement, independent of any government, political party, economic interest, or religious belief. Our activities focus on the release of prisoners of conscience. These are men and women imprisoned for their beliefs,

colour, sex, language, or religion. We try to get fair and early trials for all political prisoners, and we oppose the death penalty and torture of all prisoners without reservation.
Amnesty International has been working for over twenty years, and in that time we have helped prisoners in over sixty countries. We have won several peace prizes, including the Nobel Peace Prize in 1977 and the United Nations Human Rights Prize in 1978. Each year we handle, on average, nearly 5,000 individual cases, regardless of the ideology of either the victims or the governments concerned. Please help us, and so make us redundant in our world.

4   Drought and famine have come to Africa again this year, just as they have every year for the past ten years. In some parts of Africa it hasn't rained for three years. There have been no crops, and the animals on which many people depend died long ago. Refugees are pouring from the countryside into the towns in their desperate search for food, and it has been estimated that over 1,000 people are dying every day.
Your help is needed now. This situation is catastrophic. We need to get food, medical supplies, blankets, tents, clothes, doctors, and nurses to the area urgently. Please give all you can. No pound or penny will ever have been better spent, or more appreciated.

UNIT 12

Tapescript 33

A = **Miss Appleby's secretary**
B = **Businessman**

B   Hello. Could I speak to Miss Appleby, please? This is John Blofeld.
A   One moment, please. Oh, I'm afraid she's out at the moment. She . . .

'Write what Miss Appleby's doing at the moment.'

B I see. Will she be back in the office at 10.30?

A Let me see. Mmm. Well, she . . . *'Finish the secretary's answer.'*

B All right. She's a difficult person to get hold of, isn't she? What about lunch time? Is she free then?

A Yes, I'm awfully sorry. Just one moment, I'll check. No, she . . . *'Write what she's doing.'*

B Oh dear. What time will she be back?

A Erm . . . At two o'clock. She . . . *'Write what she's doing at 2.00.'*

B Ah. So what time can I phone back?

A Any time after 2.30.

B Are you sure?

A Definitely. She . . . *'Write where she'll be for the rest of the afternoon.'*

B OK. I'll phone back then. Thank you.

A That's all right. Goodbye.

B Goodbye.
Now listen again.
B Hello. Could I speak to Miss Appleby, please? This is John Blofeld.

A One moment, please.
I'm afraid she's out at the moment. She's visiting a factory.

B I see. Will she be back in her office at 10.30?

A Let me see. Mmm. Well, she might be late because of the traffic.

B All right. She's a difficult person to get hold of, isn't she? What about lunch time? Is she free then?

A Yes, I'm awfully sorry. Just one moment, I'll check. No, she's having lunch with a designer.

B Oh dear. What time will she be back?

A Erm . . . At two o'clock. She's seeing a customer here in her office.

B Ah. So what time can I phone back?

A Any time after 2.30.

B Are you sure?

A Definitely. She will be in her office for the rest of the

afternoon.

B OK. I'll phone back then. Thank you.

A That's all right. Goodbye.

B Goodbye.

Tapescript 34

"Groundwell" Broadcast 13.4.84, Radio 4
"Released by Arrangement with BBC Enterprises Limited"

I = Interviewer
A = David Attenborough

I David Attenborough is very gloomy about much of what he's seen. What's depressed him most has been the huge speed and scale of change that human beings are inflicting on the world. A powerful symbol of that change is the simple act of felling trees.

A In the Himalayas, for example, people cut down forests simply because there are an awful lot of people who need firewood to keep warm. And so they cut down huge hillsides, in a few years . . . are stripped of their forests.

I This leaves fertile Himalayan hills naked, unprotected from the heavy rains. The trees were umbrellas, but now the rain washes out the good soil, which ends up as mud a thousand miles away in the channels of the river Ganges.

A When the next rains come, instead of the forests on the hillside holding the rains and letting it out a bit at a time as though it were a sponge, the forest isn't there, so the rain water runs straight off and when it goes down in a huge flood; and it gets into the channels which are clogged with mud, so it then floods, so then the whole area is under water, people lose their farm land and people drown.

I So cutting down trees in Nepal drowns people in Bangladesh. In Africa the gathering of wood is making the desert grow.

A In parts of the Sudan, the desert in just 15 years has advanced sixty miles. And it's a . . . it's a . . .

devastating statistic and . . . what's more, it's a heart-breaking one, because how can you go to these people and say, 'You mustn't cut down that tree in order to cook your food'?

I But is it universally so bad? Or are some environmentalists just getting into a flap about isolated, extreme examples? David Attenborough used to wonder that, too.

A I remember very well flying over the Amazonian jungle for hour after hour after hour and not a sign of the hand of man beneath me, just this green carpet of trees. And I said to myself, 'It can't be true, it can't be true that this will disappear by the end of the century'. And so I looked into the question as to how people made these estimates. I mean, I thought, was it one of these things where you suddenly multiplied one statistic by 500,000 and you get an extraordinary answer? The fact of the matter is that those statistics are based on surveys by satellites with infra-red cameras which actually measure the change of a patch of green leaves into a patch of bare ground. And even on that level the rate at which the jungle is being . . . er destroyed amounts to about 29,000 square miles in a year.

I That's an area the size of the whole of Scotland disappearing every year. Trees are a vital part of the water cycle, and of course they give us the oxygen that we breathe. And cutting down the rain forests kills the plants beneath the trees as well, plants which help us fight disease.

A Forty per cent of our drugs, our medicines, are derived from plants and most of those come from the tropical rain forests, and most of those come from the Amazon.

I Those plants also help fight the diseases that threaten our food. The funguses and moulds that attack wheat, for example, are continually growing stronger. But they only evolve to match specific

117

varieties of wheat. So plant breeders beat the funguses by changing the varieties.

A What does a plant breeder need to change a variety? Answer – new genes. Where do they come from? Answer – wild plants. That happens with all our food plants. With rice, with potatoes, with wheat, with barley, all that applies. And if we lose those wild strains, we could well be . . . devast . . . I mean the field could be devastated and mankind would starve.

I David Attenborough insists that none of what he's said is exaggeration. It's not just a distant problem somewhere on the other side of the world.

A What we're talking about is the survival of human beings, of men, women and children. It is happening now. The floods that we hear of in India and Pakistan, the starvation that we hear of in parts of Africa, these aren't accidents. These are direct consequences of what we are talking about. And the tragedy is that the people who suffer first are the deprived people, the people who are living on the edge of prosperity. And, but if we think that we are insulated from that, that it's always going to be them, we are wrong. They are the start. As sure as fate, they are coming our way.

I David Attenborough's thoughts after seven years of travelling around the world.

UNIT 13

Tapescript 35

Toothache

A Look at this article about teeth.
B Teeth? What does it say?
A Well, apparently they've found a cure for tooth decay.
B Really? I can't believe that's possible.

A Yes. It says here we all eat far too much sugar, and that's what causes toothache.
B I know that.
A Yes, well, there's these bacteria that convert sugar into acids, and they attack the teeth and make holes in them. Well, now they've found a vaccine to attack the bacteria. They did tests on monkeys and it's completely safe.
B That's good news. How do you get the vaccine?
A It's not ready yet, but when it is, you'll get it from . . . Oh I don't think it says in the article. I suppose you'll get it from your dentist. Anyway, they're going to give it to all kids when they're three.
B What a clever idea.

Tapescript 36

Working at home

Lynn Dermott works for the Low Pay Unit. One of her particular concerns is the working conditions of 'home-workers'. These are people who can do their daily work from home, thanks to the revolution in the communications industry.

I = Interviewer
D = Lynn Dermott

I Miss Dermott, let me ask you straight away, do you think that technology has advanced so far that soon, or within a few years, many people could work at home instead of working in offices in the centre of towns?
D Oh yes. It's happening now. You see there have been such enormous advances in the communications industry, with mini- and micro-computers, and, of course, now with cable TV on its way, many people are already working from home who traditionally have had to go into an office every day.
I Mmm.
D You see, the communications industry has made more progress than any other industry in the last

ten years.
I And how do these people manage to work? I mean, what equipment do they have at home?
D Well, they have a home terminal, oh that consists of a television, a keyboard and computer, a printer, and a telephone link, to link up to other computers.
I Oh, I see. But surely there are many advantages in being able to work from home?
D Oh yes. I mean, people spend a lot of their working day actually getting to and from their place of work, never mind the expense of that, and the stress it can cause. I mean, the rush hours, as everyone knows, are the worst times of day to travel, and millions of people spend their working lives either getting up early to avoid the rush hours or or . . . travelling in the middle of them with all the pressures and stress that can cause. Something that's happened in Britain, not so much in the rest of Europe, is that people actually want to live as far away as possible from where they work. By that I mean they don't want to live actually in the centre of cities and towns. And of course the transporting of so many people causes pollution in our cities, and in general really.
I Ar yes, I see. So what is it that you don't like about the conditions of home-workers?
D What I'm afraid of is that the employer doesn't have to accept his responsibilities.
I Um . . . what do you mean? Surely the person is still an employee?
D Well yes, you may think that but let me tell you what might happen. Basically three things. One – lower wages, two – no job security, and three – poorer working conditions.
I Could you go through those one by one? First of all, why should people working at home be paid a lower wage?
D Well, indeed, but we've done surveys that show that even skilled computer operators are

paid nearly £2 an hour less than their counterparts in offices. And under British law people working at home, you probably didn't know this, have no protection against unfair dismissal, no sickness benefits and no holiday pay.

I Ah I see.

D The employer also has no legal obligation whatsoever to ensure reasonable working conditions. Now, what must be remembered is that at the moment it's only the highly skilled and well paid who are working at home. But what I'm concerned about is what's going to happen when cable networks and satellites bring down the cost of installing terminals in people's houses and then, of course, it'll be cheap enough to have all your office staff at home? Now, we think the future looks very bad for these people. For example, we've found that in the United States, companies have taken advantage of cheap communications to employ data-entry clerks in Barbados, paying them 1.50 an hour. I mean it sounds extraordinary but you think about it in those technological terms you see. In future a British firm in for example, London, might employ clerks in Belfast, or a Paris company could have their secretaries in Spain, and then they just dial around for the cheapest labour.

I Mmm. This appears to affect women more than men at the moment.

D Well, only in the secretarial and data-processing field. You see there are three million women in Britain whose jobs involve processing information, and many employers would like to have them out of the way at home, with none of the protection they would get if they were in an office.

I Yes, but surely such arrangements suit some people, particularly women? If they have young children they don't want to travel a long way from home.

And . . . uhm . . . perhaps they want the advantages of flexi-time, where they have a number of hours to do but they can choose when to do them?

D Well, of course that's true. These type of arrangements do suit a lot of women. But what we're concerned about is the question of . . . well . . . exploitation. Now, one company has given its home-workers the status and benefits of full-time employees. But you see we think this protection should go to all home-workers.
Now, what is clear is that the new technologies are radically changing the working lives of people. Well, it's those people who traditionally have had very little say in their conditions of employment. Now it would be very easy for an employer to exploit these people further by keeping them beyond the protection of the health and safety laws, and of course also beyond any possible contacts with trade unions. Now, we are in favour of the benefits and freedoms that might come with this new situation but we also want to warn people now of the risks.

I Thank you, very much.

UNIT 14

Tapescript 37

The Shipbuilders' Strike

1 Sir Albert Pringle
In my opinion, this strike is a complete waste of time – of my time and the shipbuilders' time. No worker will be made redundant. Some dockyards, about five or six, will close, because as a nation we do not have enough orders to keep them working. This industry must make a profit to survive. Men at dockyards which close will be offered jobs at other yards. I want this strike to end as soon as

possible. I have asked Mr Arkwright to sit down and talk, but he refuses. He is trying to make this strike political, not industrial, and there is real risk of shipbuilders losing their jobs if this strike goes on much longer. We are losing all our orders to foreign competitors.

2 Peter Arkwright
We are on strike because shipbuilders' jobs are in danger. Sir Albert Pringle wants to make 750 men redundant by closing ten dockyards. We can still make the best ships in the world, but this management is trying to get rid of all the workers, and soon there will be no shipbuilders left in the country. We are trying to save not just jobs but communities – towns and cities that have always depended on shipbuilding for a living. Now, I want this strike to end as soon as possible. I have invited Sir Albert Pringle to sit down and talk, but he refuses. This is not just an industrial strike. It is political, because we are fighting for the right of the working man to have a job and live in his own place of birth. My men are prepared to stay out on strike as long as it is necessary to save this industry.

Tapescript 39

A divorce lawyer

I = Interviewer
S = Jane Simpson

I Mrs Simpson, could you tell me who most often starts divorce proceedings, the man or the woman?

S The woman.

I And what is the most common reason for divorce?

S Well, the legal reason most commonly stated in the courts is adultery, but this is a symptom, really, rather than the real reason. I think there are two real reasons. One, the couple have grown apart with time, and two,

119

either the husband or wife has found the courage eventually to bring to an end an intolerable situation. More specifically, the woman's reasons are that she doesn't have to put up with it any longer, and she has grown up, become more mature, as it were and is perhaps making an important decision for herself for the first time in her life. The man's reasons are that he is growing away, perhaps because of business, and his wife who's left at home doesn't come with him either physically on business trips, but more important, doesn't develop with him spiritually.

I   You said that adultery is often the symptom of divorce, not the cause. Could you say a little more about that, do you think?

S   Yes. Adultery is not often the reason why a marriage breaks down. It's really an event that brings out the reasons why a marriage has already broken down. Adultery, you see, is a tangible fact. Many of us find it difficult to know our true feelings, our emotions, and it can be even more difficult to talk about them. Well, adultery is something you can actually point at, and say 'That's why'.

I   I see.

S   People by nature are conservative. We're afraid of change, we're afraid of the unknown, and so people put up with the most intolerable circumstances for years before coming to the decision.

I   Oh. After all your years of experience in the more unpleasant side of marriage, what's your opinion of it?

S   Well, I'm in favour of it. I think there are many good marriages. They do work, but they need a lot of work to keep them going. I think this is something unfortunately that most people just don't realize. Marriages need effort to be invested in them, just as for instance flowers need water and attention, or they die. I must say, I think it's better to end a

relationship that doesn't work, rather than stay together in misery for year after year.

I   Yes.

S   So my advice to divorcees is 'Think long and hard about what went wrong with that marriage, and so avoid making the same mistake twice.' Too many people rush into another marriage too quickly, and for example a woman who thinks she needs a dominating man but then hates being dominated will marry another dominating man, and of course it all happens all over again.

I   Mmm yes, do you think divorce should be made easier or more difficult, or in your opinion is the situation acceptable as it is?

S   Yes, it's OK. I personally think the grounds for divorce should be simplified. I think the only reason required for divorce should be one year's separation. At the moment, as you probably know, the fundamental reason is 'irretrievable breakdown', and a number of signs that might prove that. But what actually happens is that a couple knows their marriage is over, and has to find one of the accepted labels to explain it. So the present system is a bit dishonest you might say.

I   And is it true that children are the ones who suffer most?

S   Oh yes, they suffer more than we care to realize. Parents need to talk honestly to the children, preferably together.

I   Do you think then that having children is a reason for staying together?

S   No, not if the parents can't behave in an adult way. Children are a very good reason for working harder at a marriage, however, and so stopping a bad situation starting in the first place. But if the atmosphere is already tense, there will be a lot of relief when the parents divorce.

I   Uhm, tell me how you find your job? Doesn't it depress you sometimes, that you're dealing with couples who perhaps hate

each other, or who've lied and hurt other people, and are now perhaps fighting selfishly to get the most for themselves?

S   Oh yes, sometimes I'll think 'Why can't you sort out your own problems?' about a particular client. 'Be honest with yourself and the others in your life, that's all you've got to do.' But of course that's something we find very difficult. What I wish most is that they would realize just how well-off they were, and I don't mean money by the way. But when I have the client in front of me, well, I just have a job to do, and I must do it to the best of my abilities.

S   Thank you very much, Mrs Simpson.

Oxford University Press
Walton Street, Oxford OX2 6DP

Oxford New York Toronto
Delhi Bombay Calcutta Madras Karachi
Petaling Jaya Singapore Hong Kong Tokyo
Nairobi Dar es Salaam Cape Town
Melbourne Auckland

and associated companies in
Berlin Ibadan

Oxford, Oxford English and the Oxford English
logo are trade marks of Oxford University Press
ISBN 0 19 433555 0
© Oxford University Press 1986

First published 1986
Eleventh impression 1989

Phototypeset in 10½/12pt Times by
Tradespools Limited, Frome, Somerset,
England

Printed in Hong Kong

The publishers would like to thank the
following for their permission to use
photographs:

Apricot Computer (UK) Ltd
Associated Newspapers
Austin Rover
BBC
Anthony Blake
Peter Carmichael/Aspect
J Allan Cash
Channel Four Television
Stephanie Colasanti
J A L Cooke & Michael Fogden/Oxford
  Scientific Films
Donald Cooper
Daily Express
European Parliament
Financial Times
Robert Harding Picture Library
The Illustrated London News
IBM
The Kobal Collection
S & O Mathews
Chris Moore
Picturebank
Popperfoto
Press Association
David Reed/The Sunday Times
Rentasnap
Rex Features
Scottish Television
Mark Shearman
Sporting Pictures
Sunderland Echo

Swedish Railways
Thames Television
TVS
Ulster Television
Elizabeth Whiting & Associates

Illustrations by:
David Ace
Chris Burke
Andy Bylo
Mel Calman
Ian Dicks
Joanne Fisher
David Haldane
Martin Honeysett
David Loftus
Angus McKie/The Sunday Times
Gerald Mynott
Jim Robins
Kate Sheppard
Peter Till

The publishers and authors would like to
thank the following for their kind
permission to use articles, extracts or
adaptations from copyright material:

Cosmopolitan: Someone, Somewhere Has
  You Taped by Peter Freedman
Daily Mirror: Bobby Kennedy's son found
  dead
The Daily Telegraph: Wife who could not
  stop spending
J M Dent & Sons Ltd: Warning by Jenny
  Joseph from Rose in the afternoon
The Guardian: Scots in Sweden upset by
  cheap jokes, Kennedy son dies
Good Housekeeping: Run Your Way to
  Health by Oliver Gillie
Human Resources Institute: So, how long
  will you live? from Lifegain by Robert F
  Allen and Shirley Linde
The Lawn Tennis Association: Extracts
  from Children in Sport
The Standard: Mary will not be giving up
  smoking, Nurse Nicky nears her peak of
  fitness, Toothache may bite the dust
The Sun: Kennedy boy drugs death
The Sunday Times: A life in the day of
  Linda McCartney, How Ruth made
  history at Oxford.

The following listening materials were
released by arrangement with BBC
Enterprises Limited:

Interview with Mrs Olive Gibbs (Woman's
  Hour)
Educating Children at Home (Woman's
  Hour, Education Otherwise)
Interview with Sir David Attenborough
  (with the permission of Hugh Sykes,
  presenter of the BBC Radio environment
  programme Groundswell).

The publishers would like to thank the
following for their time and assistance:

Mrs Olive Gibbs
Health Education Council
National Westminster Bank

Midland Bank
The Central Council of Physical
  Recreation

Studio and location photography by:
Rob Judges
Mark Mason

The authors would like to thank Ruth
Gairns and Stuart Redman for allowing
them to read the manuscript of Working
with Words – the Guide to Teaching and
Learning Vocabulary; and also all authors
of the standard reference books, but
especially Michael Swan Practical English
Usage.

The publishers would like to thank all ELT
establishments of the French Formation
Continue who kindly participated in the
planning of this book at the early stages of
writing.

Institut Français de Gestion, Lyon
École Centrale de Lyon
Institut Nat. des Sciences Appliquées,
  Villeurbanne
Université de Lyon II
Université Claude Bernard, Lyon
Université de Lyon III
E.L.S. Paris
Totale Formation, Paris
Cours Hamilton
Formalangues, Paris
Polytechnicum, Lille
C.U.E.E.P. Ville Neuve d'Arcq, Lille
E.N.S.A.M. Laboratoire des Langues,
  Lille
C.C.I. Roubaix
C.C.I. Valenciennes
C.C.I. Le Havre, Dunkerque
I.F.G. Paris
I.L.C. Paris